Paul and Peter

Meeting in Jerusalem

Kenneth Cragg

The Bible Reading Fellowship

First published 1980

© Kenneth Cragg 1980

BRF Book Club No. 7

227.4X
C843

82042810

British Library CIP data

Cragg, Kenneth

Paul and Peter. – (Bible Reading Fellowship.
Book club; no. 7).

1. Bible. New Testament. Galatians I, 18
I. Title
227'.4'06   BS2685.5

ISBN 0-900164-52-2

design/print Eyre & Spottiswoode Ltd

Contents

1. Saul and Simon: Paul and Peter **5**

2. Jesus and Galilee **17**

3. The Way of the Cross **37**

4. The Church without Frontiers **55**

5. The Name of the Lord at Jerusalem **76**

Study Points and Questions: at the end of each chapter

For
the
Cathedral
Builders
of
Cairo
where in part
it was written:

Ishaq Musaʻad, Bishop
Awad Kamil Fahmi, Architect
Derek Eaton, Provost

1: Saul and Simon: Paul and Peter

'After three years I went up to Jerusalem to see Peter', Paul writes in Galatians 1:18. An ecumenical occasion indeed! Disciplined imagination has a rich field of study and enquiry as to what they talked of during that lively fortnight of acquaintance and debate. It quickly becomes evident that the encounter symbolises – and no doubt involved – almost all the major issues that belong with Christian fellowship and with New Testament scholarship. If we could only add St John we would have a conversation embracing the whole range of the definitive Christian mind as the New Testament, our basic Christian document, has enshrined it. However, whether in Jerusalem, Ephesus or Rome, no recorded incident brings together in a single concert of mind that trio, the Petrine, the Pauline and the Johannine.

But here in Galatians we have the two whose days together at Jerusalem, if we can truly share them, will initiate us steadily into the meaning of Christ and the making of the Church.

'To see Peter' is an intriguing phrase. The Greek verb has something of the English sense of: 'I must see a doctor', or: 'I'll see the boss for you'. Paul was not going just to learn what Peter looked like, or merely to make his acquaintance. They certainly did not talk about the weather. 'To visit Peter' some translations run; 'to consult' with a view to learning his opinion and, if possible, enlisting his authority, is the meaning. The term is well known in classical Greek and some have guessed that there lies behind it in Galatians a Rabbinic practice whereby eminent authorities were sought out in order to have the benefit of their judgement and, if given, the authority of their support.

Paul's eagerness to recruit the knowledge and seek the concurrence of Peter is all the more notable because Galatians is so emphatic that Paul needs no authority other than his own commission by the heavenly vision on the Damascus Road.

'Have not I seen the Lord?' he asks; and that experience makes other support for his vocation superfluous. That vision, he believes, was a direct action of God 'revealing his Son in me'. As Paul received it, that vision constituted him one of the apostles, even though he lacked Galilean discipleship. He may have been in that sense belatedly recruited, and so 'untimely born' (1 Cor. 15:8). Yet of his legitimacy as an apostle there could be no doubt. He was insistent that Galatians should understand so. He was not an interloper, neither was he purveying hearsay, nor was he a second-hand person needing to be attested by some more reputable figure. Fractious folk in Galatia should realise that his apostolic status, and so his pastoral authority, were not to be impugned. All this is very clear from his passionate independence of spirit in handling the tough matters that had emerged in the Galatian church.

Nevertheless, he did care about Peter and Peter's mind. He wanted his angle on all that concerned the faith and the fellowship. So we can be sure that the meeting was spirited and frank. For Peter also had his 'status' as a leader of the Twelve and one of the three closest intimates of Jesus. Paul's visit paid obvious tribute to this status by singling him out for consultation. Neither party there was likely to have been mealy-mouthed towards the other. Their sharply differing biographies to date left many potential sources of suspicion or wariness between them. So, by the same token, it must have been a full-blooded encounter, forthright and thorough.

So, in turn, it seems well to use both names of both personalities to have it in right focus as an intensely human dialogue. Saul, anyway, had not yet acquired the name of Paul, as briefly and oddly noted in Acts 13:9, where it is linked with the incident involving Sergius Paulus, the deputy at Paphos. (The Hebrew *Sha'ul* is much further from the Latin *Paulus* than the English names would indicate.) The change may itself have been part of Paul's 'western' direction of life and activity. We do not know how far the name Simon remained current, or the double name Simon-Peter. Acts consistently prefers the Petros name which Jesus had bestowed on Simon at a critical juncture in his discipleship and

Jesus' mission. (Matt. 16:18). For this was certainly the name which belonged prophetically with the founding and the building of the Church.

But Peter's 'rocklikeness' was very much a paradox of grace. There was also shifting sand in his nature, as none knew more bitterly than himself. During their fifteen days together Saul was to learn the Simon story as tenderly as Simon the Saul saga. In their exchange of 'things past' they joined together the earliest days around Capernaum with the Damascus drama: Andrew finding Simon and Ananias finding Saul; Jesus persecuted in the synagogue at Nazareth and in the Church by Saul; Jesus stopping short both Simon and Saul in their rejection of his way as Messiah; Saul and Simon alike experiencing Jesus' resurrection as their rescue from their embittered selves. The events, that had made them what they were, were full of contrast. But they had a common quality and a mutual significance. Jesus' intimate friend and Gamaliel's pupil; onlookers in the trial of Jesus and in the martyrdom of Stephen; as far apart as Galilee and Tarsus; as close as brothers – they embody in themselves the experiences that made the New Testament.

There is, of course, the difficult practical question of chronology and the sequence of events as reported in the Acts and outlined in Galatians, and not only the sequence but the details. For the two sources, with their different standpoints, do not readily tally. It seems clear that the sojourn in Arabia, referred to in Galatians 1:17, and from which Saul returned to Damascus, must be fitted into the 'many days' of Acts 9:23. Some have supposed 'Arabia' to denote a desert retreat not necessarily far from Damascus. Others like to think it to have been the Mount Sinai region, which would be symbolically appropriate to one so vitally related to the Jewish Law. How long the visit lasted is not clear. The Damascus residence which it interrupted lasted three years in all. If Saul's reappearance in the city aroused the conspiracy which threatened his life, we may guess that the Arabian period was relatively long. Otherwise it would be hard to understand why such violent hostility as was aroused by his conversion stayed dormant so long.

Saul's absence in Arabia has no recorded history. We can only assess its meaning from the thinker he became. The drama of conversion was, in fact, less dramatic than we sometimes imagine. For the vehemence which it halted already concealed a disquiet growing stronger by his very efforts to suppress it. The significance of the heavenly vision, namely that Jesus was the Christ, was there already in the confidence and constancy of those he persecuted. The blinding light and the voice from heaven had only made the surrender irresistible. His physical prostration and the aftermath of so intense a climax needed time and perspective. These could only be found in withdrawal.

It was out of that search for bearings and for new beginnings that he came at length from Damascus to Jerusalem. According to Acts he associated with the apostles, after Barnabas had reassured them about his bona fides. Paul in Galatians, concerned with the case for his independent authority, mentions only Peter and James as leaders whom he 'saw'. His intention may be to denote, not general mingling, but explicit theological consultation. It may be that some of those among whom 'he came and went' (Acts 9:28), still felt a diffidence about 'risking' him wholeheartedly despite Luke's natural instinct to describe a wholesome harmony. Other apostles also may well have been absent from Jerusalem in the widening circles or interludes of mission. In any event, Luke's narrative is sadly condensed and built upon a much more general scale of interest that Galatians. The narratives converge in their note of his departure to Caesarea and thence ultimately to Tarsus via Syria and Cilicia (Acts 9:30; Gal. 1:21), presumably by the long coastal route.

It appears from Acts that the fortnight lodging with Peter was preceded, or followed, or even punctuated, by encounters with the Hellenists in the capital. These were probably the Greek-speaking Jews of the dispersion – possibly those who spoke only Greek – and not to be confused with the Greek-speaking Jewish Christians of whom Stephen had been one. Luke, with his tantalising neglect of detail we would be eager to know, does not explain what kindled such hostility on their part against Saul.

Was it that having their own version of Jewish/Greek cross-culture, they bitterly resented Saul's interest in bringing Christ into that amalgam? Was it that Saul was feeling his own way beyond strict Jewish confines and was aroused by what he saw as their syncretism? For there was never any doubt of his loyalty to the law of Moses for the Jewish-born. Was it that they knew from Tarsus who he was, and despised both his recent rigorism and his new extravagance? Was it that they saw in Saul a powerful new recruit to the 'Christian' Hellenists who had started the Samaritan mission; and whom they deplored as having substituted the folly of Jesus crucified for the 'wisdom' of their adopted culture?

We do not know. Our concern is with the mood and the matter of Saul's consultation with Simon. It seems as clear as Luke's brevity will allow that Jesus, his story, his 'believers', the faith, its expression, the law and the Gentiles, and apostolic vocation were all in vigorous review and that the mood was urgent.

Before we come in the following chapters to a possible reconstruction of these topics, it will be well to preface them with some remarks about issues which lie behind them all and which constitute perennial items in ecumenical debate and Christian fidelity. We can well set them in three pairs – authority and experience, the corporate and the personal, and the past in the future, or faith and development. In Saul's consulting Simon we may read a symbol of these three themes deeply involved in all biblical study and in doctrine and life throughout the Church.

In coming to Peter, Paul was bringing the private to the public, charisma to community and faith to origins. Fruits were, in his coming, being related back to roots. In souls, fruits and roots are far more complex than in soils.

As we have seen in noting the motives Paul stresses in Galatians, he stands squarely on his own experience as in need of no further ground. With mystics all down the centuries, he insists that he knows. The risen Lord spoke to him in the way. That vision stays with him continually thereafter as the sole sufficient persuasion and mandate for his faith.

Such strong personalism has always characterised authentic Christianity which cannot be stated without personal pronouns. That 'the Son of God loved me and gave himself for me' is not concluded from argument or taken on trust from dogma. It does not 'stand in the wisdom of men' and is not a logic of the schools but of the heart. It is a meaning which has 'found' the soul that knows it, a gospel that decides the mind that loves it. Saul/Paul is the constant example in the New Testament of this rugged inward confidence. 'Let no man trouble me. I bear in my body the marks of Jesus' (Gal. 6:17). For all that comes to him is grist to his experience, so that as a disciple he is in fee to no one but the Lord.

Even so, he seeks the tradition within which alone his experience occurs. He 'needs' Peter – a Peter who is not to be ignored and whose standing serves a custodianship which requires to be acknowledged. The several aspects of this we will take up later. The immediate point is the right interplay of what comes only in inwardness yet belongs also with outward sources, which in being deeply private is also clearly public. The all-sufficient vision itself was entirely dependent on the real Messiahship. Saul could not be arrested for a victorious Church except with the history of a suffering Christ served in a community ready for the cost. Saul is in debt to Stephen as Stephen is to Jesus. His conversion only happens in a context through which men are made convertible – a context of grace, of history, and, therefore, of tradition.

In turn, that tradition belongs with other men's personal discovery, different from Saul's but no less intimate and private. Simon, too, has been in Gethsemane and come alive again in Easter. He has given the lie to Jesus, differently from Saul's negation of him, and has learned how to disown his own disowning.

The fact that all experience is truly personal and inward, far from exempting or absolving us from community, returns us into it more totally; for community is the reservoir of all other experience, made accessible in common witness. If Saul, out of Damascus and Arabia, has need of Peter and the public faith, so does all inward faith wherever found. Only so is that corporate fidelity itself renewed by the steady access of its living cells.

In seeking the authority that Peter represented, Saul himself foreshadows what, in Galatians, he already claims: namely, a new exercise of 'office' to which fresh personal convictions must, in their turn, relate. New believers would one day make him their Peter, their referee and mentor; or, if they did not, he would firmly require it of them. For Damascus visions can be turned into preaching only as they accept to be commended in the form of convictions that have a structure of doctrine and community.

The making of Christians is only through the inwardness of personal discovery but the Christians so 'made' are known as such by the corpus of tradition, the authority of faith by which the name they bear is defined. There are, doubtless, difficult and stressful points in history about this 'tether' of identity in creed and form, and the rope of discipleship that is tethered there. But that the inward and the corporate must be so is the truth which Paul and Peter in their meeting signify.

Paul himself was to need this emphasis when he came to deal with the charismatics in his own pastoral charge. The immediacy they claimed, their direct experience of the divine Spirit, he could well appreciate. But he firmly resisted any élitism, any dispensing with the rest of the fellowship, any repudiation of the corporate life, any disqualification of others to which such exalting experiences were, or might be, prone. He insisted on intelligibility, on the edification which required it, on relevance for all as opposed to spirituality for some. In that sense his own original deference to Peter was an early parable and sign. Indeed he 'commends' the Corinthians, 'for always keeping (him) in mind, and maintaining the tradition (he) handed on to (them)' (1 Cor. 11:2, NEB). He wanted them to realise that there is no spirituality more in danger than the one which believes itself exceptional or self-sufficient. The demonstration, not to say the discovery, of truth stands in the corporate reference and the will to unity.

Saul and Simon in their human openness to one another and in becoming Paul and Peter in their apostleship symbolise, too, the kindred problem of faith and development. In seeking out the first disciple in Jerusalem, Saul the convert was returning to origins – origins we will explore in chapters 2 and 3. But Paul was also to become a far-reaching 'developer' of what he received, as indeed Peter was himself, if in a somewhat lesser degree. All discipleship is this way. For there is nothing static in the life of grace or in the love of truth.

Ahead of both men lay the enormous revolution by which their Jewishness learned to participate in undifferentiated humanness, by the incorporation of Jew and non-Jew alike into a race-transcending fellowship across the cultures of men. Also ahead lay the development of that network of pastoral oversight by which the churches were held in one and the one was diversified into the many. Ahead, again, were all the theological lessons which could be learned only in the experience of evangelism and expansion. Historians enjoy a hindsight by which to see these changes. Protagonists have to live through them.

It is this fact of development, fulfilling origins yet leaving them behind, which is the school of loyalty. It cannot be evaded. 'To live is to change and to be perfected is to have changed often.' There is no denying that Christianity has undergone comprehensive development and that its expression in every generation takes to itself accents and features beyond what earlier generations knew or recognised. Yet what endures throughout is the abiding faith. The debates and tensions within that durable and developing reality are the very stuff of loyal discipleship. They can never properly be escaped by retreat into some supposedly immutable fixity. There are, nevertheless, always those who would wish to insist that nothing should ever be thought, phrased, or done, for the first time.

Paul and Peter needed each other precisely for this ever-present reason in the Christian fellowship. In differing ways they were each party to a vocation in and beyond faith's origins. At the time of their meeting, the great criterion for the debate and itself a product of it, namely the New Testament Scripture, did not yet exist. Their fifteen days tête-à-tête in Jerusalem had the benefit of no 'epistles'. The very churches which were to receive them did not yet exist. There were no gospels. It is impossible to say precisely how far collections of Jesus' sayings, or liturgical recital of his doings, or other forms of what was to solidify into the Gospels, had yet passed into currency. The vital process of documentation was itself within the living flux which needed it. When it happened it possessed all the features of place and context to which history is bound and which interpreters must patiently acknowledge and explore.

When it emerged, that New Testament documentation provided a lens, as it were, upon the origins it presented – a lens which, through the later Canon, affords the primary criterion for everything Christian. As such it focusses the past that gave it being according to its own measure. That measure enjoys the status of Scripture. But the authority within that status still requires of us a search behind it which realises what its own context was. For no status can exempt a text from context, or a document from its development. We do not rightly possess it unless we are intelligently related to its origins. To know what it means to have it, we must be ready to see how New Testament Scripture itself is a significant stage within 'development' and receive its authority accordingly.

This means that we both go behind it to understand, if we can, its genesis; and forward with it to fulfil its expression of the Christian faith. That expression has a primary, but not a dead-hand, control over the future. For it did not itself come by a dead-hand imposition. On the contrary, it grew with the growth of its faith and in the living society of believers. We will be wise to see in the Paul-Peter interview a sign and symbol of a faith with origins that is a faith with a future. Such is the purpose of these pages.

The basic creative work of Christian theology, we may claim, is within the New Testament. But the historic Creeds are not, except in the sense in which chemical elements are *in* a solution before the catalyst 'precipitates' them. Christmas, as a celebration, dates only from the fourth century. It is a long way from Paul to Aquinas and further yet from Aquinas to Bonhoeffer. Christian worship has been within Doric and Corinthian pillars, under soaring Gothic arches and beside screens of ikon splendour or of wattle poverty. Endlessly varied is the style of sermon from Chrysostom to Andrewes, from Luther to Moody, from Ambrose to Phillips Brooks. Clearly, there is no finalising the tenor or the temper of the faith in some unchanging cast or form or shape. Nor does language, within itself or between its neighbours through translation, admit of fixity of term or phrase. Not even the columns of the dictionary are immune from the wastage of archaism or the redundancy of usage.

There are, of course, always loyalists and diehards who must suspect and fear the flux of time and the obsolescence of terms. Their consciences must be respected but their timidities must be repudiated. There are no doctrines which can safely be left to any single metaphor. We must accept that there is a duty of adequate paraphrase of every belief we hold. For if we are not prepared, or not able, to say what 'Son' and 'substance', 'One' and 'only', 'Trinity' and 'Spirit', 'heaven' and 'holy', mean as other words might say their meanings, then the words have likely become bare formulae behind which we shelter either an empty or a rigorist mind. Even the word 'God' as a term does duty for a whole variety of ideas, notions and impressions, which honesty needs to clarify and denote with more intelligence and reverence. Being articulate to a doubtful or a wistful world is the first condition of a vital faith. There are signs in our late twentieth century that some creative rephrasing of the faith within the Scriptures is painfully developing among us. Some lively imaginative fellowship with Peter and with Paul, no less, may help us to be ready for it, without panic and without shame.

For to be ready, soberly, humbly, with expectant loyalty, is our truest emulation of the first Christians themselves. Still without gospels, other than their memories, theologies other than their convictions, structures other than their bonds in Christ, and assets other than the love of Jesus, nevertheless they ensured for all unfolding centuries the fulness of the Lord.

It is that quality which we study in the Simon who became Peter, in the Paul who was Saul, whose fortnight in close communion may help us possess our past and face our future as the double strand of one loyalty.

There is one intriguing question. Where did they meet? There seems some historical ground, as well as poetic justice, in thinking of the one 'upper room' as the 'Christian' headquarters in the holy city, as the location alike of the first Eucharist and the first Whitsuntide.

The narratives in Acts suggest a customary rendezvous to which Peter returned from prison and where the group normally foregathered. Was 'the goodman of the house', as identified by the pitcher-carrier, none other than Barnabas himself? Mark, his nephew, could well have been the young man in the incident (recorded only in Mark) who followed Jesus to Gethsemane and avoided arrest by slipping out of his night attire when soldiers grabbed him (Mark 14:51–52). So it seems fair to guess that he had been roused from sleep when the disciples trooped out of the house and had stealthily followed them in haste to learn what was afoot.

So, without being dogmatic, we will let imagination free and see Saul and Simon playing host to Paul and Peter in the very place where Jesus had first celebrated the new 'Passover' in his blood; and where the Holy Spirit filled all the house, lighting upon each disciple in tongues of fire.

Study Points and Questions

(1) 'Simon, I'm Saul, back in Jerusalem . . .' Let your imagination take the conversation on from there and see where it takes you.

(2) Paul, in Galatians, is ruggedly independent. Yet he comes to confer with Peter. Why?

(3) For the Christian, faith is always intimately personal and cannot be stated without personal pronouns. Yet it is a faith which stands only in corporate tradition. How are these two facts reconciled?

(4) Jerusalem – Damascus – Arabia – Jerusalem – Tarsus. Can you explain the spiritual sequence in Saul/Paul from hostility to persecution, to conversion, to withdrawal, to community, to mission?

(5) Examining your own experience, do you find personal convictions loosening away from traditional authority? Or do you find yourself relying on the latter at the expense of any lively possession of the former? How can you bring the two into better harmony?

(6) The apostles, with Peter and Paul in the lead, certainly 'developed' the faith. Later came the New Testament and 'documented' apostolic 'development' at its first-century point. What is our vocation, in loyalty both to that definitive document and to our own obligation for present 'development' in Christ?

(7) 'Let every man bear his own burden'; 'Bear ye one another's burdens' (Gal. 6:5 and 2). Apply these two commands to both Simon-Peter and Saul-Paul in their meeting, and judge what they might mean.

(8) Can you satisfactorily reconcile the chronology in Acts and in Galatians? Need it affect our study of the meeting?

(9) We need not think of the conversation wholly inside closed doors. Take it out to Bethany, to Gethsemane, to Olivet, to the garden by Golgotha, and give imagination to your earshot.

2: Jesus and Galilee

It seems intelligent to suppose that a prime motive for Paul in seeing Peter was to learn about Galilee or, rather, about Jesus, as Galilean discipleship had first known him. The intriguing question here is whether Saul had ever encountered Jesus anywhere directly. But he certainly had not experienced the Galilean ministry or the thrilling sequences that began in Capernaum and ended in the capital. The fact that Saul had not companied with Jesus, and so lacked that vital credential of apostleship, was a major factor in his desire to claim the Damascus vision as amply making good his lack.

But, if so, it was clearly of a different order. 'The heavenly vision' was not of Gennesareth and loaves and fishes. The voice from heaven was not the quiet humour and wisdom of the parables. Paul needed initiation into all that Peter was so well equipped to share and so to satisfy Paul's 'quest of the historical Jesus'. The two weeks' conversation in Jerusalem would be all too short a time in which to overtake two years or more of crowded event and lively teaching within the Gospel ministry.

So obvious seems this explanation of Paul's intention that it is surprising to discover much New Testament scholarship totally denying it. Paul, we are strangely informed, was completely uninterested in how Jesus had been. He was only concerned with what is abstractedly called 'the Christ of faith'. There are long book-shelves of theology setting out this view. Paul emerges for some as almost the arch-villain in the genesis of a mystic or a credal Christianity which either ignores or embroiders, distorts or disowns, the actual Jesus in the interests of a belief structure which is independent of history as it may have been. On this view, the event of the gospel is not what happened: but the believing of what was believed.

It seems extraordinary to the layman that this folly should

17

have been seriously entertained. To get the matter into focus we need to consider a passage where the issue has its departure, namely 2 Corinthians 5:16. Paul writes there of a time from which, as he says, 'we know no man according to the flesh'. This cannot mean that he has no personal friends whom he recognises by their features. He then goes on to say that though he has (or may have) known Christ 'according to the flesh', from now on he does not know him that way at all. The final climax to the passage is that 'in Christ all things have become new'.

Fascinating as it is, we can leave aside here the question whether Paul, as Saul, had ever set eyes on Jesus before the crucifixion. It is in no sense impossible, seeing that Saul had certainly travelled from Tarsus and studied in Jerusalem during the life-time of Jesus. There were also notable Rabbinic schools in the Galilee region. The question need not occupy us here, since it is not personal acquaintance with Jesus he is talking of. Moreover, unless we take his plural 'we know' as a kind of personal plural, he is joining the Corinthian readers in the statement. It is highly unlikely that any of them had kept company with Jesus, cosmopolitan as the northern territory around the Sea of Galilee may have been, and ubiquitous as Corinthians, as port citizens, doubtless were.

Clearly Paul is concerned with some other than visual acquaintance. He speaks of 'the Christ', not of Jesus, of an 'office' rather than an individual. (It was the other way round outside Damascus as we shall note later.) He is not in any way speaking about contact with Jesus. Still less can he intelligently be read as disowning all interest in 'the man of Nazareth'. Paul's alleged unconcern about Jesus 'in the days of his flesh' finds no warrant in what he says to the Corinthians.

He is telling them that he no longer assesses people and their possibilities by worldly standards. There is nobody whom he writes off as being useless material for grace or whom he sizes up by such questions as: 'Is he well-born?'; 'Is he cultured?'; 'Is he Jewish?'; 'Is he even literate?'; 'Is she decent?' For all such questions suggest limits to the renewing, transforming potentialities of grace anywhere in society.

This non-despairing, non-despising, stance is because Paul's ideas of Messiahship had been radically altered since his introduction to Jesus as the Messiah. We do not now identify Messiahship, he says, by worldly standards. We do not see him realised in nationalist style liberation; in Essene style austerity and withdrawal; in Sadducean political *sagesse*; in Zealot militarism; nor even in that scrupulous piety which finds him so ideal that it must concede he never comes. We do not know the Christ these ways – ways which embody the pride, the anger, the fear, the malice, the restlessness, of men. To have identified 'Messiah crucified' – a favourite phrase with Paul – is to have left behind these unworthy but still popular criteria of who and how he would, he should, be.

Aspects of Paul's meaning here will concern us again elsewhere. The present point is to disavow the idea, based on this passage, that Paul had no deep interest in the Jesus whom the disciples loved and followed in Galilee. Quite the reverse: we take his fortnight with Peter to have been a further effort on his part to make good his ignorance and to overtake his lack.

'The heavenly vision' which some think absolved him of such interest in fact necessitated it. To have seen the Lord in glory was no substitute for the lowliness whence that glory came. Nor should we misunderstand what some have supposed to be the 'silence' of the Epistles, arguing that Paul was negligent of Jesus' teaching in not citing it more freely.

There is, of course, wide and continuing research into the formation of the New Testament and into the relationship of its two main genres of writing, namely gospels and epistles. The former, as a unique sort of document, were in embryo and in development within the Church, in oral and in written sources. Their formation was in progression with the emerging life, dispersion and definition of the community of faith. It seems clear that the Gospels were the expression of the Church's retrospect to Jesus as that retrospect receded with the lapse of time and the passing of the initial generation. There is never any doubt of the instinct and the duty within the Church to tie back their existence to the facts of Jesus. We need not exempt Paul from that general circumstance of both church life and literature-formation going on all around him, and in which Luke, one of his close associates, was vigorously engaged.

The Epistles have a different métier. They are concerned with the pastoral nurture of the Church, its ethical guidance in the dubious world, its spiritual direction and self-understanding. The two broad types of document need not overlap, given their concurrent purposes and their immediate genesis, whether rapid as with some letters, or prolonged as with all the Gospels, in the growing Church. To conclude disinterest in Jesus from silence in the Epistles would seem to be a misconstruing of what New Testament literature is.

And certainly the silence is far from complete. There are clear echoes in Paul's writings of the words and accents of Jesus. 'There is nothing unclean of itself', he tells the Romans (14:14) and directly attributes the quotation by saying: 'I know and I am persuaded by the Lord Jesus'. The whole tenor of the passage is reminiscent of Mark 7:14–19, where Jesus stresses that 'uncleanness' is 'within', not outside, a person. The very word here *koinos*, being a somewhat strange usage, warrants our thinking that Paul has a verbal tradition in his mind, and not merely an association of ideas. He asks also, in the very idiom of Jesus, 'Why do you judge your brother?' (Romans 14:10; Matt. 7:1–5; Mark 9:38–39; Luke 6:37–42). 'Giving account to God' on an individual basis was a clear emphasis made by Jesus (Romans 14:12; Matt. 12:36). Paul returns to the theme in 1 Corinthians 8:13 about 'the stumbling block' in another's way (Romans 14:13) and to the Romans gives the Gospels' term, *skandalon*, a good Greek synonym to press it home.

Did Jesus' reference to the 'baptism (he had) to be baptised with' (Luke 12:50) inspire Paul's own repeated association of baptism with self-giving in 'death'? Metaphors like 'heirs to the kingdom' belong with Jesus' parables and with Paul's Rabbinic parallels. When he invokes 'the grace of our Lord Jesus Christ' upon his friends and readers why need we suppose that he is oblivious of the middle word in the triple name? Then, perhaps deepest of all, there is the portrait of love in 1 Corinthians 13 and the strong conjecture that its descriptives derive from the personality of the Beatitudes.

The aim here is not to exhaust Pauline mindfulness of the earthly Jesus but only to reject, for the distortion it is, this notion of Paul's indifference. The way is now open for imagination to pursue the Peter/Paul encounter as an occasion of participation in vivid memories of Jesus. Peter's was surely a retrospect ardently renewed, Paul's an appetite keenly urgent. We will consider later the matter of Paul's Christology and its relation to the Jesus-history. For, in rejecting the misconceptions just reviewed, we have not fully reckoned with the Jesus–Paul relationship.

But before we can appreciate the pattern of Christhood, as achieved by Jesus and affirmed by Paul, we must dwell in the Galilean hills and villages with Jesus as Peter and the others had known him. That is where it all began. 'Jesus came into Galilee, preaching the gospel of the kingdom of God' (Mark 1:14).

We will be wise here to sense the impact of either on the other in their conversation. Lively conversations turn on the initiatives that each takes. Otherwise there is monologue and audience: friendship degenerates into a lecture. Rich conversation evokes a mutual expression, kindles the fuel of either's mind in the flow of the other's interest and the fire warms both hearts. Peter was more qualified than any to tell the Jesus-story, few more calculated than Paul, fresh from Arabia, to draw the story out. If history is surest when it is, as we say, 'existential', then Paul was the perfect foil for Peter the narrator, and Peter the perfect interpreter for Paul.

The visitor had been passionately implicated in the sequel to the narrative. His zealous persecution of the nascent Church had been continuous with the violent hostility that had developed against Jesus' teaching; and which had finally engulfed his person and his band of followers, with Peter at their head. That passage into tragedy Peter had survived, even though traumatically. He had been witness to all but its last climax at the Cross. All its antecedents in joy and spring gladness, in crowd exhilaration, and in private intimacies, he had fully experienced as they unfolded around him. Reliving them for Paul was re-enacting them for Peter.

A glance here at that moot point about whether Paul as

Saul possessed any independent experience of Jesus is appropriate. Some scholars have made an eager case for the affirmative: others are sceptical. Paul's only reference, in 2 Corinthians 5:16 is, as we have seen, indecisive. It seems likely that, if he had really known Jesus, he would have been explicit about it. It is true that, in Galatians, and elsewhere, he was emphatic that 'the heavenly vision' constituted him an 'apostle', though 'born out of due time'. That the Damascus mandate sufficed, however, need not require us to argue that he was, therefore, deliberately suppressing some other occasion of 'seeing the Lord'. For, clearly – and this is the crucial point – any such 'seeing' of Jesus 'in the flesh' was in no way a discipleship. At best it would have been casual, at worst hostile. So, on every count, we must conclude that there was nothing antecedently in Saul's biography which could have satisfied the interest which had now brought him to Peter's door.

If there had been prior acquaintance, it would only have left either prejudices to be undeceived, or second-hand impressions to be filled with life. Nothing is surer about Saul the persecutor than that he had never met the Jesus whom Peter knew until that Jesus spoke from heaven.

So Peter's role in the conversation was vital. The two, in this area of their meeting, were not comparing notes. Simon could be interpreter to Paul because his part in the history had been crucial. He had been the prime member of the inner circle of three, spokesman often of the twelve, son-in-law of the household which would appear to have housed the original 'Christian' movement in Capernaum and, most of all, in some sense a foil for Jesus himself.

We have perhaps been too ready, in our attitude to Jesus, to lift him out of all relationship to the disciples save that of leadership, authority and 'mastery'. Matthew in particular conveys this impression of lordly self-sufficiency, of total spiritual autonomy that hardly needed disciples at all, except, as it were, for *their* sakes. We need to have the picture truer, and Mark gives us many a hint. Jesus called his disciples 'that they should be with him' and not only that 'he might send them forth to preach' (Mark 3:14). He was deeply concerned about how they regarded him and he leaned heavily upon their loyalty and love. He genuinely needed them. They were no mere retinue for a lonely self-sufficiency.

It is evident that Peter must have a special place in this truer picture. Was he not, in measure, the human partner in whose exchanges of thought Jesus himself found his own way through the crises of his work? This is certainly so at Caesarea Philippi, about the suffering Messiahship, as we must see in chapter 3. But from the beginning Peter may be said to have known something of the inwardness of Jesus as well as the outward story of the ministry. It was out of this interior knowledge that he 'educated' Paul.

It is tempting to think of that education into Jesus of Paul by Peter in terms of the summary of love in 1 Corinthians 13:1–8. It is feasible, imaginatively, to explore by those very emphases. The imagery there, after all, is about gifts in 'the body of Christ' and there is a conscious analogy in Paul's theology between the ministering hands and lips and walk of Jesus *and* the corporate action and character of the living Church. 'Members in particular' in the latter may correspond with features in particular in the former.

Jesus came teaching; Jesus came healing. His 'ministry' of those gifts had an eloquence and an efficacy subdued to love. He spoke of faith 'moving mountains' (Matt. 17:20) and of giving goods to feed the poor. But he made it clear that the alabaster box of unstinted devotion was more acceptable than all routine almsgiving, love being the supreme condition. 'First be reconciled' was his prescript for acceptable liturgy. For all its admired excellence, as Peter knew from the felt adulation of the early crowds, Jesus' teaching was always within reach of the common people who heard him gladly. It had no place for that kind of *gnosis*, or élitist knowledge, which Paul's hymn to love later condemned. There was about the parables none of that subtlety cherished by people of ecstasy or esoteric insight, who vaunted their uncommon status. By contrast, it was a teaching shot through with simple goodness and a compassion for the simple-hearted in their ordinary hopes and fears. Pride of *gnosis* was to be a constant threat to 'the simplicity that is in Christ' (2 Cor. 11:3), the sincerity Paul earnestly coveted for all his own disciples in the run of human frailty. For all such was 'a rejoicing with the truth'.

As a recent Pharisee, Paul must have catechised Peter about Jesus' relations with his former mentors. How had Jesus really handled that vexed question which dogged Paul's whole thinking, namely the just pride and the necessary reproach involved in divine law? How had he really squared his readiness for 'publicans and sinners', even prostitutes, with his duty to the law? For law must surely disavow the deeds which flout it and, because of them, the people who defy its prohibitions and deny its commandments. Surely love failed here, if it ignored the necessary loyalties of law, neglected law's obligation to penalty and requirement to condemn. Law can, perhaps 'hope all things' before it has been flouted. But how can it 'bear all things' when they cry out for retribution?

Here Peter's perception of Jesus reads almost like an anticipation of Paul to Romans, but for the Galilean accent. Jesus was 'justified' in Zacchaeus – a story which epitomises the whole of Paul's later argument. The end of the law, that is, its goal and purpose, was a righteousness of the will. As a positive, law witnessed to this. Hence its undoubted place and worth in the economy of God and in the realising of a true humanity. But, as a punitive, law had to concede that its end was defeated. Jesus, therefore, refrained from condemning. He hoped all things from the Magdalenes of this world; invited himself into the hospitality of Zacchaeus and his kind; stepped outside the pattern of rejection of them. So doing, he kindled hope in the fallen and drew them to the penitence which then 'justified' his attitude and action; thus bringing about what law existed to identify and realise, namely 'righteousness'.

Paul was later to grasp this insight exemplified by Jesus and to turn it round from the 'justification' of love in its action to the 'justification' of the sinner by his amenability to grace. Faith, of course, is present on both counts. With Jesus there is the 'justification' by faith of the love-relationship in that it broke through the hard heart, opened a way out of the inhibiting shame and communicated an active hope of a feasible new start – what Paul was later to name 'newness of life' in Christ. With Paul it was the 'justification' of the sinner in terms of that new status before God, the end of reproach and the beginning of holiness and liberty from evil.

Alike for Jesus in the Gospel and for Paul in his Epistles, there was no further reason why law should decry that experience, or impede that result, by stubbornly 'requiring that which is past'. On love's view, law's consistent concern for retribution for the past is the sure factor spelling frustration in the present. Does not the good life, *via* grace and penitence, in fact fulfil the law's end? Why should it then be disallowed because it abandons the law's means? Are not means anyhow for the sake of ends? While Peter ruminated on Jesus' activities, Paul may well have been brooding on the ways of God. If the Epistles are any clue, however delayed, to what passed between them, it is because the conversation proved a seedbed of the theology. Can we say that in part Paul became the pastor he was through the discipleship that Peter had recounted?

Of course, love – in Jesus, or elsewhere – has its particular failures. 'Justification' is not automatic success. There remains the mystery of the hardened heart. To say that 'love never fails' in contrast with things that wane and cease is to say that it is the perennial thing, the pattern that nothing will supersede. The reason for his policy lay, as Jesus saw it, in the fact that this was the way of God himself. The parable of the father and the two brothers was there, from Jesus, to prove it. 'Far countries', for Jewish ears, and swine's diet, were certainly circumstances of estrangement from God, of enmity to God and to law. The younger son had obviously nothing to commend him prior to knowing that he had nothing. But at that very point, the father's unbroken relationship, his patient suffering over the wanderer, came into their own. To these the exile could return and, because of them, return to the ring and the robe and the feast.

This, for Jesus, was the nature of God – the nature that warranted and inspired a like practice on his part, in exciting and in trusting penitence. The point about the elder brother is that the father quietly presses upon him – perhaps unsuccessfully – the same readiness for love. 'This your brother', the father says to him, gently reproaching the alienation the elder son packs into the phrase: 'This your son . . .' Whether he finally owns his relationship with the wanderer we do not know. Many of the later issues in the Jew/Gentile Church are here and may explain why Luke preserves the story. For the Gospels, we must remember, have their content and their authorship responsive to the current situations to serve which some historical retrospect was sought. Peter and Paul in converse were only on the threshold of that future. But as much, and more, than many others, they were part of it.

Running through their conversation, too, we may be sure, was the fascination of reflection on the character that underlay this realist, and yet serene, teaching. For the message of the kingdom had somehow been inseparable from the kingliness of the messenger. Not a tyranny of dominance in any sense, only a quiet authority which subdued strife among disciples yet tolerated their diverse temperaments. The kingdom had borne with their very rawness for it. Peter, with his impulsiveness, had many occasions to recall this quality in Jesus. It reflected the sort of grasp on reality which breathed in those Beatitudes. These, as Peter realised in quoting them to Paul, were not promises about some distant future. They were statements of present fact. 'Happy *are* ye when men shall revile you', only stated what was true about the 'love that is not easily provoked' and 'thinks no evil'. The solid happiness of the poor in spirit belongs to the love that does not seek its own. More joyous than all mystic wisdom is the insight of the pure in heart. The blessedness of the persecuted could hardly fail to come home to Saul with his near memory of a persecuting past. Had not Ananias and Barnabas been happy peacemakers whom Saul himself had learned to call children of God? In this his own desperate way the persecutor himself had been hungering and thirsting after righteousness and had now in truth been filled. Paul's own narrative must have enriched those Beautitudes for Peter also.

But the teaching authority which could speak in these terms with this superb confidence – how was it to be explained? It was an authority which respected traditional institutions yet made their purpose sometimes override their form. The Sabbath, for example. Jesus kept it religiously 'as his custom was'. But he steadily refused to make the needy victims of its incidence. 'The Sabbath', he insisted, 'was made for man, not man for the Sabbath'. He did not fear, as others might, the question: Who, then, is to decide what its subordination to human ends requires? This was the question legalists were liable to avoid in a dull loyalty that was also cowardice. Jesus, by contrast, had a simple confidence in One he called his 'Father' – a confidence which enabled him to counter the traditionalists with firm assurance: 'But I say unto you . . .'

It was a hard, and perhaps yet unresolved, struggle for Paul to enter into that same liberty of creative, critical, allegiance to the past. Peter had less difficulty. For, as a fisherman, a layman, he had never been a rigorist. With Paul, Jewish privilege, Jewish uniqueness, Jewish institutions, Jewish fidelities, would continue to lay a sharp burden on mind and conscience. Only as a Roman was he 'freeborn'. Only with a great sum – of heart-searching – did he obtain his religious freedom.

Yet he could understand readily enough that, seeing the Sabbath was made for man, its benediction of perspective and rest was entirely secure. The saying of Jesus about it was no magisterial dismissal but a more intelligent and positive avowal which his practice had confirmed. Law was more truly an end under God because it was no longer an end in itself, as its own guardians had the instinct to make it. Was it not the permanent temptation of religious authority to turn truths entrusted into powers exercised? Structures of control were then in danger of usurping the very ends they supposedly served – a state of affairs which could be challenged only by the novel and radical alternative: 'But I say unto you . . .'

That shock of rethinking had another consequence as well as breaking free of static traditions and official attitudes. These involved not only a rigidity in the office-bearers but a conformism in the community. Where prescripts were sacrosanct, obedience was likely to be of the letter, and externally merit-seeking. The new inwardness which Jesus demanded of the law's custodians he required also of their people. Hence the emphasis on the inwardness; the intention; the will that underlay the surface of performance; to detect the lust within the propriety; the lovelessness within the almsgiving; the pride besetting the piety; the worship which congratulated the worshipper.

Such common temptations to the inauthentic, present even where men are most religious, were to remain a concern of Paul's pastoral mind. They also dominated his own personal struggle for purity of heart as analysed in Romans 7. Peter had much to tell him about how that '. . . but I say unto you . . .' had searched the disciples' motives and, on many occasions of friction, false ambition, or mutual strife, had revealed them to themselves and helped them towards maturity.

Through all the unfolding of Peter's recollection, as Paul's intense curiosity prompted it, there ran an underlying theme which is central to the whole New Testament. It was the way in which the gospel *of* Jesus became the gospel *about* Jesus. The passing of the one into the other is the genesis of the Christian faith and constitutes the birth of the New Testament. Paul, 'seeing' Peter, was in a real sense finding out about that development in the reverse direction. He was coming to Peter – if we are right – for the Galilean past but doing so out of the meaning of the gospel about Jesus and from within the Christ of faith.

It is our conviction here that there is a genuine unity between the two phases and that this unity of the New Testament, disputed as it is in many quarters, may be given a lively symbol in the apostolic conversation we are pondering. Certainly Simon and Paul brought together in their persons the poles of the ellipse in the ministry of Jesus and the Church of the Epistles.

Everything begins where the Gospels place it, in 'the prophet of Nazareth of Galilee'. Jesus comes preaching the word, the news of the presence of the kingdom of heaven in the here and now. The call is to repentance and faith. The teaching is evidenced by healing; the healing is interpreted by teaching. This, in word and deed, is the gospel of Jesus, the good news of God, the blessedness of trusting him and being in his world.

The personality of the teacher/preacher proves to be inseparable from his doctrine. The quality of authority which, as we have seen, belongs vitally to the message, inevitably focusses attention on the person: 'I say unto you'. The message never ceases to speak to free intelligence, to human feeling and to common sense. It uses parables from nature and from home life which the simplest of folk can understand. Its appeal is to day-to-day experience. 'What man of you . . .?' it asks. The listener can readily assent for himself to the logic that is offered. In all these ways the word is no arbitrary hand-out, as if its acceptance were merely submission to a dictating authority. The personality of Jesus does not override his hearers' minds.

Nevertheless, there was no separating his personal relevance from the relevance of his wisdom. 'Come unto me and I will give you rest' centred the kingdom's invitation round himself. The yoke that spelled rest was his yoke. That he was 'meek and lowly of heart' was somehow significant for how his listeners might become so too.

Inevitably, therefore, the gospel of Jesus developed into the gospel about Jesus. The crucial stages of that story lie outside this chapter. For they turned upon the Cross. The ultimate stages lay outside the New Testament altogether in the theology of the Fathers. Peter's memory and Peter's reflections were intimately concerned with all its scriptural phases – phases which certainly belonged in Galilee where, in Paul's catechism of him, we stay in this chapter.

We can hardly do better here than return to those Beatitudes. For what became central for Peter was not things said, memorable as they were, but Jesus saying them. What emerges most of all from the Galilean ministry is the comradeship of men, of disciples with a master. Their sheer variety made their unity no accident, no easy accommodation. There was a former tax-gatherer in company with Zealots – Simon the Zealot for sure and probably Judas Iscariot also. The sons of Zebedee were 'sons of thunder', temperamentally explosive chaps, with surly Samaritans around to rouse them. And there was the morose and languid Thomas. Had Jesus been 'easily provoked' he could hardly have held this ungainly group together. Could he have chosen them in the first place had he not 'hoped all things'? All his patient tuition of their natures was a steady 'rejoicing with the truth'.

They were cumbered, too, with many false ideas of what they were about, with ideas of eschatological sceptre-wielding. Priority of rank was hotly debated among them. But, in retrospect for all of them, and not least for Peter, was the power of a personality practising the love of man. Had they not fed the multitude from the loaves and fishes? Did Peter now regale Paul with the story of that incident and the vivid memory of companies, gay like flower-beds, stretched neatly across the green grass? Or the occasion when he had wanted to dismiss those superstitious women with their babes in arms seeking *barakat* from the touch of Jesus? The master had rebuked his impatience despite his doubtless sounder views of what the kingdom meant, and had sided with the popular notions of the power to bless, pathetic as they were. 'Let the children come to me.'

Unlike Peter, Paul was unmarried and there is nothing about childhood in his writings except where he exhorts it or turns it into a parable of Christian meekness. But Peter, perhaps remembering those nursing mothers, wants his readers thirsty for 'the sincere milk of the word'. The incident, however, if recalled or not, fell into a general pattern, where lepers and lame, the blind and the broken, were welcomed to his compassion. There can be no doubt that the precedent of that shepherding, as experienced by the disciples in themselves, and in their partnership with it, was the inspiration of the pastoral quality which characterised the apostolic Church.

When the disciples became apostles they achieved by travels and by letters something of the active caring which Jesus, in the Palestinian setting, had sealed into their memory on occasions without number. 'I am persuaded by the Lord Jesus' (Romans 14:14) covered much more than rubrics of cleanliness and food. It inspired and guided Paul in 'the care of all the churches'. (2 Cor. 11:28). The very phrase he uses there about an onrush of claims and demands ('that which cometh upon me daily') is reminiscent of the pace and crowdedness of Mark's Gospel.

As a fellowship of human concerns, in the education of disciples who were to become apostles, the ministry of Jesus made his personality decisive for their experience. He taught by being who he was even more than by saying what he said. The Gospels, written all in retrospect, show this very clearly. It must have been different while it was still in process. But even if we try to divest ourselves of hindsight, it remains clear that the disciples were more and more confronted by things *about* Jesus as being implicit in the things *from* him. What needed to be said about him grew steadily from what was taught by him.

The New Testament is itself the witness to that double situation. The Gospels were *wanted* in the Church. There is, through all development, this resolve to tie all back to the actual Jesus. The faith never takes off into unconcern for its Galilean origins. It is a faith which writes the Gospels because it is a faith which treasures Jesus. Yet those Gospels themselves are from within convictions about him as the Christ and the Lord, without which they would neither have been wanted nor produced. They are witnesses *to* history only because they are witnesses *from* faith, and they witness *to* a faith only because they go back to a history. All the questions of New Testament religion are in this situation, in what has long been called 'the quest of the historical Jesus' — a quest which must always be 'with the historical Church'. We cannot have the witness and elude the witnesses.

Despair or distrust about this situation has led to two contrasted attitudes. One is to depreciate the historical altogether, as it concerns Jesus and to make central the historical as it obtains in the Church. In other words the *preached* gospel, quite apart from its sources in Jesus, is the great historical fact, the fact of a heralded faith. This must be taken independently of what may, or may not, have preceded it and which, anyway, is (they say) irrecoverable.

The second attitude is to look for some Jesus who can be

had, as if he had not generated any historical Church, a Jesus retrieved from all such development seen thus as distortion, aberration, deification or fantasy. The Jesus so retrieved may be 'Jesus the Jew' (in a sense which wills to isolate one central fact as if it alone was definitive), or Jesus the liberal, Jesus the Zealot, Jesus the charismatic, Jesus the meek, or simply Jesus the enigma. These versions are liable to cancel out each other. They reflect the predilections of the 'retrievers'.

This second handling of the Galilean story suffers the strange discrepancy of failing to explain why the retrieved Jesus should have generated the – on this showing – aberration-picture of faith. It may suggest reasons – sheer credulity, religious inventiveness, pagan precedent, pietistic wistfulness and the rest. But, with all these suggestions, goes the basic puzzle. How could an aberrant Church so marvellously have bettered Jesus himself in crediting him with a quality which, on this showing, he did not possess – the quality of setting at the heart of Messiahship and of Sonship to God the clue of a love that redeems?

For there is no doubt – as we shall study in chapter 5 – that this is the decisive and distinctive conviction of Christianity – God in Christ, and Christ via the Cross. If, then, Jesus was not the great originator of this truth, the Church unaided must have been and, being so, bettered Jesus himself. The Church itself becomes, on this view, its own originator. Its generating truth is its own genius for interpretation. What we have then to do is to go back behind that origination to the real facts about what was interpreted. We must, as it were, dismiss Hamlet, and go back to look for Shakespeare. Some enigmatic association between the two somehow persists (for after all there *are* the Gospels). But we must detach the authority of Jesus from any 'authorship' (in both senses of the word – genesis of community or documentation of faith) of the Church. We cannot rightly suppose that he ever either intended, or effectuated, it.

The first attitude to the Galilean story, namely that which makes the essential fact of history that of the Church alone with its faith, creates a different kind of puzzle. It makes the Church's faith self-generating in a different kind of way – not because the original Jesus, when retrieved, disowns it or detaches from it, but because he is himself irretrievable. The Jesus-the-Jew, Jesus-the-liberal, Jesus-the-Zealot accounts, which properly ought to engage us seriously for their concern with history, are really so much futility. The faith of the Church is so much in the way of the recoverability of Jesus that it is pointless to try to get behind it and recover him. Faith, anyway, can never be the result of the successful solution of a detective mystery. The Galilean ministry is not one we can dependably retrieve. But this need hardly deter us. There is no reason why it should worry us. The *kerygma,* as the Greek word has it, the word announced, this certainly is history – Peter preaching at Pentecost, Paul reaching Rome. What matters is the conviction that in the Christ God had acted. By this conviction men today are still being confronted with that by which they can interpret their own existence and are challenged to live by what it demands of them. Answering that challenge is the summons of faith. It neither needs nor undertakes the quest of any Galilean enigma. Such academic abstraction misses the real point of confronting life now in reliance upon the God who meets us in the gospel and the 'Christ in us' who is 'the hope of glory' (Col. 1:27).

This understanding of faith, however, is less than honest with the content of the gospel on which it chooses to hinge decision. In that gospel 'Jesus came preaching'. It is important to know what he said. We do not have a revelation in the Holy Spirit which needs no Holy Scripture, any more than we have a Holy Scripture which needs no Holy Spirit. 'Our Lord Jesus Christ' was the loved form of New Testament devotion and we may not well neglect any one of the three words that comprise it. Christhood and Lordship are in and from the original Jesus. But the Jesus we follow is a Jesus in whose life and word and character and relationship with God are the roots and birth of the Church.

This is not to claim that Jesus intended all that the Church has been, or has become, in history. Yet even to disown all disparities and betrayals, we must know where the criterion returns. It *is* to say that we must loyally hold together the gospel of Jesus and the gospel about Jesus, the Church from

Jesus and Jesus through the Church.

To see it this way is to have the clue to what is generally called 'Christology' – a word which often puzzles the ordinary Christian. It has generally come to mean that study which tries to define the nature of Jesus and which uses abstractions like 'of one substance with the Father', and ventures into philosophical formulation of the way in which the divine and the human participated in the person of Christ. Paul himself had some part in this formulation, notably in Colossians, where his people seemed to call for it by their fascination with esoteric knowledge. The early Fathers of the Church carried it very much further and with ever more conscious subtlety of mind and phrase.

But primarily, for Paul and also certainly for Peter, and for ourselves, Christology has to do with the art of being the Christ. The art of Messiahship is fulfilled in the actuality of ministry, in the activity of encounter with the evil of the world, in the living care of truth, in the acceptance of pain; and finally in the bearing of sin as the world in its sinfulness brings love's travail for it to the climax of crucifixion. This is Christology – not Chalcedon with its formulations, but Gethsemane and its prayers. Likewise, the 'Sonship to God', which figures so centrally in 'Christology', has to do with a deep, actual, filial fulfilment of the divine mind in the human situation, before it reaches verbal definition in the language of dogma.

The deeds of the Messiah and of the Son are prior to the definitions, the doer to the dogma. Prior to all is the reality and character of God from whom all is derived. All must, therefore, be kept – and be seen – within theology: within the love and power of God, making good in Christ – in this Christ – his fidelity as Creator to the humanity he created; his consistency as the lawgiver with the world he chartered for his glory; his commitment to the risk of man. It is because God is the God he is that the Christ, his active disclosure in history, is as Jesus is.

We must be careful that we test all our Christology, as terms for doctrine confess it, by Jesus' achievement of it, and that we see his Sonship to God in that unity of will that made

34

achievement real. We must stay close to Christology as Jesus realised it, in the living world that stretched, so briefly, so inclusively, from Galilee to Jerusalem, from baptism to resurrection.

Throughout this chapter we have been seeing Simon and Saul, Peter and Paul, as meeting in these meanings, actually in retrospect and recollection, prospectively in reflection and brotherly exchange. The Acts always refers to 'apostles', the Gospels to 'disciples', The development of the learners into trustees, of the recruits into the captains, was central to the whole story. They belonged with one unfolding kingdom and one redemption. Our two in their private encounter are tokens of that great transition out of a past into a future, with a past that was for a future. They were themselves a vital human link.

Rather than venture into their 'direct speech', we have instead stayed in earshot, exploring their themes as the inter-penetration of past and future, looking together unto Jesus, 'the author and the finaliser' of their faith, and of ours.

We located their conversation in the Upper Room on Mount Zion. Fifteen days would surely be long enough and their instinct sure enough to take them to Gethsemane where Jesus 'oftentimes resorted with his disciples'.

Study Points and Questions

(1) Does the argument from the relative 'silence' of the Epistles about the content of the Gospels warrant the view, sometimes held, that Paul was disinterested in Jesus as the disciples had known him? Why should such a view arise?

(2) How 'silent' are the Epistles? Look out and list echoes and evidences of Jesus' teaching in the pastoral writing of both Peter and Paul.

(3) What is Paul's meaning in the important passage in 2 Corinthians 5:16?

(4) What is meant by distinguishing the gospel *of* Jesus and the gospel *about* Jesus? How does the one give rise to the other? Was the development a right one?

(5) From your study of the Gospels what would you say were the main ethical and spiritual issues between Jesus and the Jewish priestly leadership?

(6) 'He taught them as one that had authority' (Mark 1:22). How was this so?

(7) How did Jesus 'educate' his disciples? What were the vital lessons which they had to learn?

(8) How far do you think Jesus' own course of thought and ministry was determined by the relationship with the disciples, especially Peter? How far was his gospel reflected in the choice of them – fishermen, publicans, Zealots and others?

(9) 'The pressure of Jesus' life on mine.' Being Christian was once summed up in that phrase. What is this influence to you? How do you think Peter would have summed up what it was to him as he talked with Paul?

(10) 'Jesus of Nazareth – the Christ of faith.' How should we see the relationship?

3: The Way of the Cross

Peter's retrospect to Nazareth and Capernaum and Paul's initiation into its cherished meanings, which occupied us in the previous chapter, were, like the events themselves, only a prelude to the climax of Jesus' death. We stopped short of Gethsemane. We must surely assume that Paul and Peter spent long hours talking of it and of all that followed it.

They had such different personal perspectives from which to understand. Peter, as we must soon more fully explore, was an active party in the exchanges which shaped Jesus' decision preceding it. In measure, he knew Jesus' travail, if only dimly, from within. Paul, by contrast, had been arrested by a crucified Messiah, whilst campaigning against the very notion that he could be Messiah. Each apostle needed the story of the other's journey into faith, unlike as they were, but converging on the one conviction: 'God has made this same Jesus . . . crucified, both Lord and Christ' (Acts 2:36). Let us take first Paul's 'realisation' as to the Cross.

The Damascus-road story, told three times in the Acts, is familiar enough. The voice from heaven said, 'I am Jesus'. It is there, quite certainly, that all study must begin. A voice from heaven saying, 'I am Christ' would have caused a godly Jew no surprise – awe, doubtless, and perhaps exultation that such a vision should reward his godliness, but not surprise. Was not the Christ supposed to be 'riding on the clouds of power'? A celestial figure invested with divine authority to subdue all enemies such a Christ would be. *Where* the voice spoke from plainly meant Messianic status. But *who* the voice identified – this was the altogether amazing thing. 'I am Jesus whom you, Saul, are persecuting'. It was amazing because every instinct in Saul's soul, every fibre in his being, rejected totally the claim that the crucified preacher, Jesus, was the point in history of Messianic fulfilment.

It was precisely that claim which gave birth to the Church – the community Saul was harassing for the very reason that they made this claim. 'This Jesus whom you crucified is Lord and Christ.' Hence the persecution of that community represented persecution of its Jesus, as the Christ-figure, just as the voice from heaven said. 'Your hostility, Saul, to them all is one piece with your hostility to me.' It was all of one piece, also, with that rejection by the religious authorities which had preceded and had occasioned Jesus' crucifixion. Saul's antagonism was sharpened even further by the obstinacy, as he saw it, of people who insisted on that false Messiahship after the death which, on any sober count, must have entirely discredited both claimant and claim. Priests and scribes were angry enough with what they saw as Jesus' pretensions before his execution. It was even more intolerable that they should be echoed and circulated after his grim demise. Saul, 'breathing out threats', was the ardent expression of that determined revulsion.

It is plain, then, that the vision on the road met him at the very centre of his anger and of his conviction. It insisted, against all the odds of Saul's prejudice and passion, that the sufferer at the Cross was in truth the Messianic reality just as the Christians said. We misread the story if we think that the light from heaven was totally arbitrary, altogether dramatic like a bolt from the blue, an intervention which turned all the tables. On the contrary, it was the climax of things significantly present within Saul's own struggle. It confirmed what could be read in Stephen. It belonged with the fidelity and the patience of Saul's own victims. The drama is real enough. But it was not a sudden assault from beyond. Rather it was like the breaking of a dam behind which a weight of waters had been steadily, if stealthily, gathering. Saul's violence only hides his misgiving. His indignant zeal is the way he silences his suspicion of himself. 'Lord, who *are* you? what will you have me to do?' are cries that then burst from his lips because they had been struggling within him already. The vision and the voice released them.

We can see how all Paul's subsequent theology is an 'obedience to the heavenly vision': his career, certainly, but his theology also. In his writings we find the words in every order: 'Christ Jesus my Lord', 'Jesus Christ Lord', 'my Lord

Jesus Christ'. The heart of his gospel is in that confession. The person, the office, the supremacy – these are the Messianic reality, Jesus crucified and exalted in majesty in all his significance as to God and as to man.

About Messiahship, however awaited or described, there had always been a double question: 'who?' and 'how?' (once doubt or anxiety had got beyond the question: 'whether?'). There was the person to be identified or, if not a single figure, then the agency, and there was the 'policy' he, it, or they, would follow (if so ordinary a word as 'policy' can be employed). To know, authentically, who Messiah was one needed to know how he was. To identify his action would be to recognise his identity. Jesus' contemporaries had very diverse ideas on both scores. The core of the first Christians' faith was that Jesus had been the Messiah and had been so by virtue of the love that suffered. He was Messiah crucified. The divine answer to the human situation – which at its fullest is what Messiahship means – was there realised and accomplished in the fact of the Cross.

Paul's submission had been to that reality. In the isolation of Arabia he had brooded on its meaning. But he had no insight into the course of Jesus' decision leading into such a climax. By what logic of faith, by what pressure of events, had Jesus in his ministry of teaching and compassion, moved forward into that finale which all the Gospels record and which they all see as the ultimate point of his significance?

Peter was better qualified than any, save perhaps the beloved John, to report the sequence into crucifixion as Jesus had lived it. Peter had watched it develop. He had bitterly resisted its necessity and had finally broken under its strain. He had been rescued only by the power and reassurance of the resurrection.

Our task is to enter into Peter's presentation of that experience as Paul's education into the Cross from the side of actual history. Only so could his submission to it from the side of resurrection-vision be fully intelligent. Damascus, after Arabia, had to come to grips with Golgotha.

Alert readers of the New Testament are aware that there were many forms of Messianic hope. What we have to learn is the Messianic consciousness of Jesus, where the deep questions lie. There are, we may believe, two dependable clues to them, the primary one in the nature of God and the secondary one in the precedent of the suffering servant. These two were brought into play in Jesus' decision by the way in which his ministry developed. Let us briefly look at these 'sources' before Peter takes up his story of how they transpired in the event.

That God is 'Messianic' i.e. such as to initiate what Messiah does and to intend what Messiah achieves, is implicit in the doctrine of creation and of revelation. (We will return to this in chapter 5.) To create such creatures as humanity and to summon them in law and by prophet is to be involved in their response. When that response is defiant, rebellious, wilful to the point of self-distortion and perversity, the creating lordship is itself at stake. Hence in broad terms the Messianic hope, as what God would do about man, how divine power would meet the human tragedy. Messiah would be, in action, the undefeated resourcefulness of God in respect of human wrong. 'The anointed of the Lord' would be the agent or agency of a divine answer to the 'problem' of humanity.

When that 'problem' was read as political, or communal, or economic, then a military, or a priestly, or a royal, Messiah might suffice. When it was read in deepest terms, the divine adequacy to it, as represented in and by Messiah, would have to go much further. For this very reason some believed that a Messiah could never be identified, would never actually 'come', so that he might always be hoped for. The issue in all this was how to understand the Messianic dimension in God himself.

It would seem that, for Jesus, the primary clue as to how divine lordship would act could be found through a secondary clue offered in 'the suffering servant' described in Isaiah, chapters 42, 50 and 53. This mysterious figure has been the theme of many explanations and interpretations. There are good reasons for linking it with the experience of prophets such as Jeremiah. For prophecy, by its very nature, given the evil world, runs into tragedy. Men in hating a message soon turn to hate also the messenger. Unless the messenger trims his message, appeases or quits, the hostility deepens and he is himself in danger. This occupational hazard of the faithful prophet means that suffering is inescapable. He must live with wounds and the possibility of final sacrifice. Such situations cannot be met with a reciprocal hostility, with strife and violence on his part, unless the message itself is to be tarnished and denied. He can only meet enmity with meekness and persecution with fidelity.

By those qualities alone – and their costliness – can the true prophet keep faith with the truth and so save his people. These might then come to realise how 'with his wounds they were healed', how in anger they had 'gone astray', and how under God their iniquities had come to rest on the faithful 'suffering servant'. There is nothing contrived or artificial about such redemptive pain, as if it were prescribed to fit a scheme or work a theory. All arises from within the actual situation where love of truth meets society in the wrong.

This clue to the Messianic secret had been latent for centuries, though almost completely ignored. Clue indeed it was. For if such were the case with loyal prophets, how could the central figure in the divine economy of faith expect to escape the same vocation? What brought the latent clue into centrality in the Gospels was, first, the mind of Jesus himself and secondly the developing pattern of his own life. Obviously Jesus as a teacher incurred increasingly the same experience of pain and rejection. Announcing the kingdom, he became the target of the enmity of the vested interests which resisted it, of the privilege which it threatened, of the pride which it disallowed.

Jesus seems to have sensed that he was approximating closer and closer to the pattern of 'the suffering servant'. It came to him with increasing clarity that the Messianic secret lay within that precedent of redemptive suffering and that to embrace it was the shape of his vocation.

'Messianic woes', so called, were not unknown to popular ideas about the future. It was felt in some quarters that evils would have to get worse and worse, before Messianic intervention would be warranted. Otherwise, once intervention had occurred, the Messianic solution might turn out to be premature because evil had not come to a head or finally shot its bolt. Also the more dire the situation the more total the Messianic success and vindication. Thus 'woes' might be part of the human story – the woes, that is, of those who waited, not of Messiah himself. There would be no ordinary logic in having the very source of deliverance somehow itself needing to be delivered!

There was one odd variant on this, sometimes given harbour in weary or desperate minds. It was that perhaps these 'woes' could be shortened or averted if some 'Messiah' deliberately put himself in mortal peril so as to force the divine power to intervene because otherwise all would be lost. It appears that tempting Satan in the wilderness had some inkling of these notions!

Such ideas were far from the integrity and realism of Jesus himself as the New Testament presents him. They were aberrations to reject. But rejecting them leads us back to Messiahship through suffering, Messiahship, that is, 'according to Jesus'. Here we call in Peter.

His deepest recollection, he told Paul, was exactly this 'drift' towards the tragic in his experience with Jesus. The early days and the initial discipleship had been glad, expectant, even blithe. There was light in Peter's eyes as he recalled them.

'Spring was in the air, Paul, and everywhere the sweet landscape of Galilee. To be sure, there were Roman soldiers everywhere and many harsh reminders of our servitude and poverty. But all was young and promising. The common people heard us gladly and the world seemed at our feet. There were crowds on all hands and the charisma of Jesus lifted spirits high.

'But, little by little, as the issues emerged and sharpened, we sensed a changing atmosphere. Establishment grew suspicious of the implications and passed from mild interest into strong hostility, and from hostility to rejection. Jesus seemed to sense this development, all disquieting to us, as somehow destined. He did not evade it, nor would he appease it. Rather he held all the more resolutely to his sense of mission. He began then to question us about what we thought of his impact and his "reputation", both with the ordinary folk and with the priests. He seemed to feel a fascination about

Jerusalem, as if it had everything to do with the shape of the future, whereas, for us, this harsh capital was the very place to avoid. We could see no point in leaving fertile Galilee for the city with the stone heart, the killer of the prophets.

'It was just this setting of conscious hostility that always came to the fore when Jesus talked of things Messianic. He was inclined to shun the word itself. I can see now that he had in mind the confusion we were in about the word and the idea. So he preferred to speak of himself as "the Son of Man", though this, too, was a phrase we did not well understand. But always it was associated with words like "giving a ransom", "being lifted up", having "nowhere to lay his head", and "being set at nought".

'Several of these phrases took us back to echoes in the prophets, where "ransom" and "being despised" were used of somebody called "the suffering servant". It almost seemed to us as though Jesus was finding there the meaning by which to understand his own reception at the hands of our nation or, at least, the powers within the nation. It seemed to pre-occupy him as the key to his own reading of where things were heading both for him and us.

'There was a point in our story, Paul, where all this came to a sort of crisis. We had gone further north than ever before – to Caesarea Philippi in fact, as if we were meant to get some better perspective on our mission by withdrawing from familiar haunts. Jesus appeared anxious to secure us, as it were, about who he was and then to startle all of us with quite shattering implications about how he was to be it.

'He asked us straight out about what current opinions said concerning him. What had folk concluded from all his works and words? We told him what we knew and how much of it had to do with being "like the prophets", though, as you know, Paul, we had not had any for long centuries until John came with his baptism. It's your Rabbis, Paul, with the Maccabees, who have been shaping Israel these late centuries!

'Then he brought the question really home. "Well! what did we think of him?": "What report had we to give?" It was I, Paul, who undertook to answer for the rest. I said what had been growing upon us all the time: yet somehow it had then the force of a new discovery. I told him we took him to be the Christ. His response was electrifying. It seemed to come from the very core of him, compounding both release from tension and joy of heart. He blessed me as the spokes-man of a revelation from his Father, as if he were sensing in our recognition a confirmation of his own filial mind. It was as if his being "Son of the Father" both explained and required the path he was intending to take. It was of that he went on to speak, telling us to keep our insight to ourselves and warning us about dire things ahead when he "went up to Jerusalem".

'This was too much for me. In spite of his stirring words about the Church to be and my part in it – or perhaps because of them – I challenged his talk about suffering and death ahead of him. I implored him to repudiate such thoughts and put them out of his mind altogether. "This shall never be to you", I said with all the emphasis I could muster; and I meant it, every word. I felt I was struggling to save him from himself, to secure his Messiahship and make certain that what we had only just realised and hailed should not be cast aside in gloom. What I said was really like a deep "Hosanna!" – that word we were to use later when we did enter Jerusalem. "Be safe, and save!" How could he save others unless he were secure himself?

'What I meant was that if he was thinking of those Messianic woes, well, they could fall on us. We disciples were expendable, like pawns in a game. "This shall never be to you", I repeated. If suffering had to be, let us pawns take it. For if the king is dead, the game is up. There is no saving unless Messiah himself is safe, not only safe but victorious. Truly, I wasn't clear what victory would be: but I had no mind to find it in defeat.

'His reply, once again, was vehement, even violent. He called me "Satan", no less, and said I did not understand the mind of God. Again there was that mysterious connection between how he should act and who he was, between his service and his sonship. It was clear that in my effort to divert him from that tragic path I had touched the nerve of everything he held true about himself and about his calling. He began to talk then about our taking up a cross of ours, which left us groping to understand and desperately sick at heart.

'After Caesarea Philippi the shadow of Jerusalem and what might transpire there lay darkly across our path. I remember a vivid occasion when we were on the road [Mark 10:32]. He went on ahead of us as if driven by an intense urge and the distance between us seemed a bitter symbol of how far we were from knowing what that urge meant to him. But then he stopped and waited for us to come up to him and, then, once again, he repeated his conviction about being rejected and of the anguish of "the Son of Man". He even used the very words of Isaiah [53:3] – they "esteemed him not". "He shall be set at nought", he said.

'There were times, Paul, when he seemed to want confirmation from us that he was right, when all my combative instincts were the other way. We were dogged in our loyalty but increasingly under strain because, the way he was going, we could not see how our loyalty could be worth anything to him. How were we to help "prosper" a Messiah who somehow did not want to be "prospered" in any form that we could comprehend?.

'There was one very memorable occasion when all this was at issue between us – between us and him, I mean – when he took three of us aside and we made a mountain expedition, almost like Elijah going up his Horeb or Moses his Sinai. Law and prophecy were always in our minds because it was there that all Messianic promise sprang. All at once we were in a cloud and there, radiant as light, were the very protagonists of our Jewish heritage. They were talking with Jesus in the midst of the cloud. We were rivetted to the spot in awe of the vision and were possessed with a great feeling of exultation. No words could be adequate. But what I said was how grand it was and why could we not make tents there and have those celestial presences stay with us and we with them. At the heart of my hope was the idea that they would certainly disabuse Jesus of his suffering complex and launch him upon a real path of Messianic coronation. Why else, you might ask, should they come to salute him?

'But I was all wrong. When the vision faded we were left with Jesus alone. It transpired that he was more pre-occupied than ever with something he called his "exodus at Jerusalem". In fact he made us understand that death was what Moses and Elijah had discussed with him. He told us to keep the whole experience to ourselves, no doubt lest others, hearing our story, should take it to presage some easy Messianic honour.

'So we moved on towards Jerusalem. His parables grew yet more pointedly personal to himself – not now about seed sown, and talents bettered, and the kingdom working like leaven, but parables about vineyards and servants thrown out of them and someone he called "the Son" sent into the danger and being murdered in a supreme repudiation of the vineyards' lord. Indeed, that term: "the Son of Man" grew in prominence in his conversation in direct relation to this gathering sense of suffering as vocation. "The Son of man has nowhere to lay his head", he told a would-be recruit who presented himself one day [Luke 9:58]. Was it, we wondered, just a comment about the general restlessness of humanity, the restlessness which might well deter anyone offering for a discipleship committed to humanity? Or was it not rather a clear hint that, as he saw it, the Messiah could not rest in any compact with the Zealots, or with the Sadducees, or with the hard legalists, nor could he find solace in desert solitudes where communities waited in scorn of the world for apocalyptic intervention? "The Son of Man" could only "lay his head" in loving self-giving as the evil world pursued him to the cross.

'So we made our way steadily to Jerusalem. Yet there was nothing morbid or morose about his progress, only the bitter tension in our hearts. As for him, well, there were the old flashes of humour, the old carefreeness in compassion, the old assurance of charisma, as when for example he handled old blind Bartimaeus at Jericho gate and how he stopped under a sycamore tree to call down a dapper little man called Zacchaeus, a publican, who had climbed up there, concealed in the branches to get a better look at Jesus. There was laughter as well as consternation when Jesus called him down and said he'd lodge at his house overnight.

'But for all this wonted zest and zeal, the strain was telling on us. The situation grew ever more ambiguous, he leading and we following, but in differing idiom; he intent, intense, we bewildered, loyal, vaguely straining after light, struggling against foreboding. Sabbath came and we entered the city, with all that ambiguity somehow captured in the strangest of events. He sent two of us ahead to fetch a donkey and he rode the beast into the city, as if he wanted to bring an open challenge but do so in a form which would clearly show what the challenge was. The whole episode was so altogether out of character. Always before he had shunned publicity, sent crowds away, deterred admirers from all outward demonstration. Now, so oddly, he staged one himself and, released momentarily from our phobias, we all let ourselves go, sharing with our Galilean retinue of friends and debtors of his healing, in a glad acclaim. In our exuberation we were tempted even to feel that he had shed his fears, too, and changed his tune. Our responding Hosannas did their utmost to keep him to the new turn of mind.

'But we were deluding ourselves. The hard city gave us a sullen reception. The plaudits faded and that night in retrospect the demonstration looked from Bethany like an idle effervescence. That incongruous donkey told it all. The guise was the guise of kingship but the fact was the fact of pain. The cleansing of the Temple brought anger down upon him and all the rising enmity he had always sensed at Jerusalem came to its peak in the days that quickly followed.

'We were overnight each evening in Bethany until the fifth evening. Our inner tensions were growing with every waking hour and troubling our dreams when we fell wearily asleep – tensions between tenacious loyalty and faltering confusion. It seemed more and more that an intolerable discrepancy had developed between his understanding of leadership and ours of discipleship. We were lost in perplexity about how he wanted to be followed, and how we could follow and he so full of impending demise. Had he meant the familiar ideas of Messianic "woes" preceding Messiah's manifest victory, we could have braced ourselves for them. But he was talking about tragedy for Messiah himself – a notion utterly repugnant to everything we had stood for in standing by him.

'The climax came that Passover eve. He sent two of our number to prepare the upper chamber, here in the house of Barnabas. There we shared the bread and passed the cup of hallowing. He linked them firmly with his own anguish of heart, said they were his body and his blood, which, like bread and wine, were being given for the life of the world. It was that evening Judas Iscariot left us. He had taken to breaking point the disquiet which haunted us all. It may have been that he thought to confront Jesus with a situation in which, either he would sink for ever, or be obliged to take the strong line, the martial stand, which, as Judas saw it, he had so long and so tantalisingly refused. If so, Judas terribly miscalculated. For what, on that evening, could have precipitated Messianic denouement in fact turned into Jesus' capture. The retaining fee which Judas had accepted, the thirty pieces of silver with which his Zealotry had meant to double-cross the priestly schemers, became in truth the bitter wages of betrayal.

'Judas, at any rate, had rightly calculated that Jesus would resort, as usual, to Gethsemane, to talk and pray with us in the shade of the olive groves, under the haunting spectre of the city walls across the Kedron, ghostly in the moonlight. It was there he came upon us with a band of soldiers from the priestly guard. We were numb with weariness and struggled hard against the drowsy sleep which was our only refuge from the anguish of our souls.

'At the moment of arrest Jesus was in full command. He somehow dominated his captors, preventing the arrest of all of us, and snuffing out the angry brawl which we would readily have provoked, laying about against the enemy. Seized himself, he made sure that we were free, though how we could use our freedom – with him in bonds to them – on this we had no light, only bitter, desperate agony of mind, our honest discipleship ending like this in a tragic paralysis of will.

'Paul, I cannot bear to tell you more of that fateful night. Or the morning that followed. Do not urge me to break my heart afresh in a narrative that sears my very soul. It was that I no longer knew how to follow and in the bitterness of that despair and emptiness I insisted that I had never been a follower. I could not make the lie persuade them: it was too plainly false. Even my accent gave me away. But no more could I make the truth credible to myself. Everything was undone – to think that he should come to this and we helpless, pointless, in the midst of it, reaching the supreme climax of his vocation as clearly he took it to be, and we, clueless about what might be our part other than the blankness of irrelevance and denial.

'You came here, Paul, to talk about the Cross. I'm telling you what our cross was, the misery to us of our Messiah, arrested, condemned, crucified and buried, and us, strong Galilean lovers of his every word, his cause, his voice, his face, doomed to forfeit our discipleship where we had no glimmer of its duty or fulfilment.'

The two apostles sat with bowed heads in silence. As Peter relived his agony, Paul thought upon the vision. Gethsemane and Damascus were one fabric of grace. Saul's hostility to the Christian movement was blood-brother to those marauders in the garden. So much the voice had said: 'I am Jesus whom you persecute'. But that voice came from heaven, spoke with eternal authority and joined in one the suffering Jesus of the Cross story Peter had narrated and the living Christ of the divine intention. Paul realised more deeply than before the actual antecedents of that Messianic secret in the person of the

Jesus Peter knew. Peter, for his part, knew from the presence of Paul at his side, as learner and friend, the ongoing power, the reality, of the victory he had so painfully known as a dark tragedy. The two men corroborated each other as Easter does Gethsemane. Their two contrasted angles on the Cross symbolised the past and the future of the Messianic present as it was in Jesus and him crucified. Peter's history had its climax where Paul's vocation found its origin. The two were in themselves the living tokens of the Christ-event in its antecedents and its sequel.

Their personal experiences of the Resurrection followed the same pattern. It was steadily becoming clear to Paul that the heavenly vision had enabled him to 'overtake' the lack of direct discipleship. On this he would increasingly insist as his ministry ripened. 'Have not I seen the Lord?' Yet, even so, he was 'one born out of due time', marvellously added to the family of the disciples after the days of history in which discipleship had come to be. The 'due time' had emphatically been Peter's and so it was with the Easter history. What Paul was to learn of the lordship of Christ from the heavenly setting, Peter had come to know in the garden's intimacy. He had investigated the empty sepulchre and noted the linen clothes lying significantly within it and heard the strange report of the women folk with his own ears.

Most graphic of all, he had experienced the gentle reinstatement by which he had been allowed to retract his dreadful repudiation of the Master. In direct exchange with the risen Christ the three times repeated: 'Do you love me?' had drawn from him the glad response in which he had thrown himself upon Jesus' own knowledge of what was deepest in his heart. 'You know, Lord . . . ' (John 21:15–17). In that confidence he had thrust back upon Jesus' own perception of his failure the real brokenness of his experience, the lost bearings of his all too human loyalty in the clueless crisis of Good Friday.

Now, in Easter, that cluelessness had ended. The sense of the presence of the risen Christ spelled the vindication of his choice of suffering as the final attainment of the Messianic meaning. That vindication Paul had experienced in his arrest on the persecuting road. As the two men pondered their intimate convictions, it came to them that Jesus' saying in Gethsemane, 'Let these go their way' possessed a strange significance (John 18:8). The arch-persecutor had been summoned, by the risen Lord, to desist from the harassing and impeding of the infant Church. His counterparts in Gethsemane had been required by the victim Jesus to spare his hapless followers while he 'trod the winepress alone'. The authority was that of redeeming love, continuous through suffering and victory. The security of the disciples within the tragedy looked to the future of courage and fulfilment against all mortal odds. The transformation within them, like the abiding authority behind it, was the reality of the Resurrection. *Not* resurrection as some incongruously happy ending to a story – but resurrection as the quality of the victory already present in Gethsemane, the undefeated power of the love that gives and bears and saves.

It was in this way that Peter and Paul together began to shape their characteristic pastoral theology. 'That which I also received' was a phrase Paul was to use insistently as, with all his rugged personalism, he claimed himself to be squarely within the corporate tradition. Later, in writing to the Corinthians, his fortnight with Peter enabled him graphically to recount the first Eucharist as part of his tutorship of a young and sometimes disorderly Church (1 Cor. 11:23–29). Peter, for his part, drew strength for his theology from the heightened sense of the preciousness of recollection as eager audience had confirmed it. There grew, correspondingly, in his mind a lively awareness of what he owed to all those 'who not having seen (as he had) yet had believed' (1 Peter 1:8). In this he was at one with all who possessed the intimate memories as a cherished trust for the expanding fellowship through the lapsing years. The instinct for the writing of the Gospels came to be central to the extension of the faith as the Church rooted itself in its own origins.

Peter's First Epistle, in later years, hardly makes a moral or a pastoral point without referring to 'the example of the Lord'. Humility, fidelity, compassion, are all 'as our Lord Jesus Christ has shown . . .' Peter reminds his readers that he has been 'a witness of the sufferings of Christ' (1 Peter 5:1).

His words, especially in one graphic passage, are those of a vivid bystander watching what he tells: '. . . who his own self carried our sins in his own person right on to the cross' (1 Peter 2:24). Here a theology of atonement and a sharp focus of personal memory come together in the sort of unity which is the making of the New Testament itself.

Was it during this fortnight with Peter that Paul, fresh from his brooding in Arabia, began to develop his characteristic theme of being 'dead with Christ that we may also live with him'? The full intensity of Romans no doubt still lay in the future. But already, when he was telling the Galatians about his 'consulting' with Peter, he was saying: 'I have been crucified with Christ, nevertheless I live . . .' (Gal. 2:20). Was he even in Jerusalem beginning to see the parallel between 'death' and 'baptism', which he was later to emphasise and to link that parable with the actual death and resurrection of Jesus?

Then the death of Jesus on account of human sin – such as Peter's narrative had graphically underlined – would be seen as the believer's death *to* sin in that, realising the costliness of salvation, the Christian would take Christ's death *for* sin as his own *to* sin. Then, in turn, the Resurrection became the symbol and means to a new life in which evil was overcome. Paul was then able to insist that receiving the forgiveness men had from Jesus' dying for them meant also accepting the verdict of the Cross on their sinful selves, its reproach of their selfishness. The Cross is to be seen as something in which they had participated in the proxy of the perpetrators themselves.

This interpretation naturally assumed a direct emphasis on the historical actuality. But it did so, not in terms which would incriminate only those historically involved, to the exoneration of all who, in time and place, were not party to the event. On the contrary, the event had an inclusively incriminating character for Jew and Gentile alike, humanity past, present and future. Christ 'died for all, that they (all) who live should not live unto themselves, but unto him who died for them, and rose again' (2 Cor. 5:15). 'God concluded all under sin', and of that sin the Cross, for all time, had been the central evidence and sign.

It was in this way that, through Peter's mediation of the story, Paul was able to see in right perspective his own personal rejection as the persecutor. To know the actual cross was to know oneself the more deeply guilty but also to know oneself no longer exceptional but part of a wayward human whole. Paul found liberation on both counts – the liberation that was a new bondage of love and surrender. His teaching about baptism draws heavily upon this imagery and the analogy between baptism and death opened up a reciprocal analogy of physical death as also a baptism into life. For just as the believer surrenders his life, spiritually, to be no longer his own but Christ's, and so finds himself possessed of a different self; so, in physical death, he may likewise consciously forgo his being in order to find it again eternally. The conjunction of all that meaning in Christ with the calendar Passover, as Peter had narrated it, in his story of the last days with Jesus, only made more impressive the nature of liberation in Christ. Waters of baptism became symbolic of the Red Sea passage into liberty.

It would be idle, of course, to credit to the fifteen days with Peter all that the mind of Paul later comprehended. But it would be wrong to mistake the deep potential of the encounter for the shape and assurance of his thought.

Out of sheer crippling perplexity and bitter unwanted treachery, Peter had been rescued by a Messiah who saved others in not saving himself – just the reverse of the confident formula in which Peter had understood and pledged his loyalty. It was only in appearance that cowardice had been his undoing. Behind it lay this unnerving experience in which Messiahship could only be achieved by a revolutionising of every conception of it, every expectation about it. Peter and his fellow disciples could only know the meaning of their trauma of shame and bewilderment once they were beyond it.

They had thought they had in Jesus the Messianic person: but they had been strangers to the Messianic pattern. Their agony was to have been caught between *who* Messiah was and *how* he was. They were following Jesus in terms which he was sent wholly to transform. Peter, in the very following, had been an active partner in the issue. But he was only able to yield to the master's mind about it in the aftermath of his achievement of it. His denial in the porch of the High Priest's house was the last, the violent, form of his steady dissuasion of Jesus from the way of the Cross. By its very nature that Cross was able to contain that disavowal and overturn it in the restoring, redeeming power of its patient love.

Saul's denial of the crucified, while still a stranger to Peter's experience, had fastened on the community that confessed his secret. Peter's 'dialogue' with Jesus had been eagerly excited in a sharing of the Galilean spring-time of the story, then deepened in the darkening shadows of the Jerusalem road; Saul's was nourished in the pride of law and the status of authority, doctrinaire and distant from events. Correspondingly, it had been brought to climax in an experience of countermanding authority – a celestial authority which had authenticated the Christhood of Jesus with heavenly witness.

'Seen of Peter', 'seen of me': Paul was able to record the two experiences with the same word, thereby joining himself with all that Peter had known and witnessing to his own drama as truly one with the fellowship of Peter and the nascent Church.

Travelling from Jerusalem to Damascus one is liable to go through Galilee, and, returning, likewise. Conversing with Peter in the capital Paul was reliving both his own journey back from enmity into faith, and that of Jesus forward into Messianic climax. But of neither journey was Jerusalem a terminus, only the point of departure for the ends of the earth.

Study Points and Questions

(1) Why was it that when Jesus came to die he had no disciples at all?

(2) Within Saul's experience on the Damascus road, explain the significance of the fact that the voice said: 'I am Jesus'.

(3) 'You can only know *who* Messiah is when you know

how he is.' (The person and the pattern identify each other.) Explain how this was so for the disciples, and for the apostolic faith.

(4) How do you think we should understand the Messianic vocation in the consciousness of Jesus and in his reaction with the disciples? What were its sources in prophecy and in Sonship?

(5) 'This shall never happen to you' (Matt. 16:22). What did Peter mean, and why?

(6) Why do you think Paul was so fond of the analogy between baptism and death? What did it mean for him?

(7) Both for Peter and Paul the reality of forgiveness springs directly from the suffering of the Cross. How would you answer a puzzled outsider who asked how the death of Jesus, these centuries ago, can relate to my sins, or my forgiveness, now?

(8) The term 'a Christian' is taken, of course, from 'the Christ'. What, in simple but comprehensive language, would you say is the relation between them?

(9) The gravitation towards the Cross in Jesus' ministry (which Peter sketched here) might have been halted or reversed by (a) Jesus trimming his teaching to avoid the worst; or (b) the disciples becoming 'men of violence'; or (c) divine intervention (as with Abraham in Genesis 22). Why were all these excluded in the mind of Jesus and the mind of God? (Peter and Paul will guide you to the answer.)

4: The Church without Frontiers

Central to the Saul/Paul conversion was the Jew/Gentile equation in grace. It is important that we explore how the logic of grace opened peoplehood-to-God to all mankind on the simple ground of faith, quite indifferent to race or culture. Wary as we need to be about the agreed conclusions that Peter and Paul may, or may not, have reached, there can be no doubt that the world and its undifferentiated inclusion in the gospel figured largely in the exchanges of the fifteen days.

The historian in Acts writes, no doubt, with the benefit of hindsight. Yet even so, the future is potential in the past and to record retrospectively does not exclude foreseeing prospectively. Hindsight provides the confirmation rather than the logic itself. From the beginning Paul's conversion is seen to involve that breaking out from Jewish exclusiveness which his apostleship heralded.

Ananias is sent to him with the simple greeting: 'Brother Saul', and the promise that he, Saul, is to bear Christ's name to the nations. Each of the three narratives in Acts (9:15; 22:21; 26:17) includes this 'sending far hence unto the nations' as an integral part of the opening of his eyes to faith. Paul himself in the Letter to the Galatians makes the same emphatic point: 'It pleased God to reveal his Son in me . . . that I might preach him among the heathen' (Gal. 1:16). Much heart-searching and many vicissitudes lay between the Damascus vision and its fulfilment as far as Illyricum and Rome. But there is never any question that conversion and commission are inseparably connected, and that the commission goes explicitly and insistently beyond 'chosen people'.

It is urgent to understand how Messiahship according to Jesus is Messiahship for the world. Peter was probably not ready for this logic when he met in Jerusalem with Paul. For better confirmation, his reluctant conversion to universality stood in experiences of his own and not in Paul's ardent argument.

But what lines must that argument have followed and how may we understand that this was no unilateral enthusiasm? Still less was it an aberration of Paul's. Rather it was the inner compulsion of the Church's own emerging faith as to God in Christ. Happily, the very first initiative to embrace Gentiles on equal terms was taken by certain nameless disciples from Cyprus and Cyrene (Acts 11:19–20), in Antioch, while the main thrust of this development, both in action and concept, belonged with Paul.

It was the Cross which made the difference and Jesus' extension of 'the suffering servant' pattern to Messiahship itself. Clearly any traditional view of Messiahship would be wholly exclusive to Israel, or strictly dependent on Israel for its benefits. Zealotry, certainly, looked for a nationalist liberation from Roman power and schemed for a military salvation which would have renewed the power of the Maccabees, as it had been before the fall of the Jewish State. There was nothing universalist about that vision of the future.

Indeed, it required for its militarism a direct reversal of the meaning of the suffering servant in Isaiah 53. So perplexing and intolerable had those ideas become that the Targums, or commentaries, actually reversed the sense of the text so that the sufferings, far from being borne redemptively, were inflicted on the enemy. 'He was led as a lamb to the slaughter . . . he opened not his mouth' became 'the mighty of the peoples he will deliver up like sheep to the slaughter . . . there shall be none before him opening his mouth.' For 'by oppression and judgement he was taken away', the glossing commentators read: 'Out of chastisements and punishments he will bring our captives near'. Instead of 'for the transgression of my people was he stricken', they substituted: 'He will cause the dominion of the Gentiles to pass away from the land of Israel and transfer to them the sins my people have committed'. So, finally, 'the travail of his soul' and his being 'satisfied' turned into the people's deliverance from subjection to the nations and, 'looking on the punishment of those who hated them', the people's being 'satisfied' with 'the spoil of kings'.

Such a reversal of the sense of the Isaian anticipation of a suffering saviour was current throughout the Aramaic-speaking Judaism of Jesus' day and of the early Church. Messiahship in terms of such reversal would clearly have related only punitively to nations outside Jewry, while it satisfied and toughened the nationalist exclusiveness of such a Messiah's people.

Where there was an awareness of universal implications within Messiahship they were understood to entail some sort of submission to Israel as the price and condition of inclusion. The Gentiles would benefit as a by-product of the sovereignty which Israel would enjoy. Their inclusion would never be on equal terms or a common ground. The 'royal' Messiah of some Jewish futurism would certainly dispense favour and control destinies beyond the confines of Israel; but within those benedictions there would be no sharing of the instrumentality.

When the Messianic was envisaged in priestly terms, whether singly or in partnership with a 'royal' Messiah, the Jewish particularism was even more marked. For a temple Messianism involved the ritual of sacrifice, of blood purity, of right ancestry, of circumcision, and all the rigour of the law and the covenant. These are necessarily excluding factors. Birth is a sharply definitive event which cannot be subsequently reversed. Many obstacles hedged the way of those who might seek a sort of naturalisation to overcome the accident of one's genesis. The law was strictly associated with the 'seed' of Abraham and ancestry in 'Moses' and the Exodus. Sinai was a particularising experience.

Only the Noachic covenant of seedtime and harvest, summer and winter, day and night, belonged to all mankind. Unifying as these basics were, they did not avail against the separating uniqueness of the Torah which only Israel possessed. It was the Torah, in the land, which hallowed those natural sequences and interpreted the material economy and the social situation they afforded. Thus the divine privacy between God and Israel was a most cherished element in a tenacious feeling of identity. This unparalleled physical and theological corporateness of Israel was the most fundamental fact of Paul's experience and it certainly dominated all popular Messianic hopes.

Sometimes those hopes inspired a rigorous withdrawal from the world, even of ordinary Jewish society, let alone from Gentile corruptions. Communities like those of Qumran in the Judean wilderness believed that the Messianic future could only be inaugurated when the time was fully ripe in God's design; and that, meanwhile, as a precursor of that climax, human history must descend into even darker evils. From these the pure in heart must scrupulously withhold themselves to prepare for divine intervention by an unsullied exemption from the deeds of darkness. That perspective also pre-supposed that salvation and Torah-people were inseparably united.

All these differing forms of Messianic hope, with their common emphasis on the Messiah's own people, involved the basic question of the law and its observance. Here the exclusiveness of righteousness within the law was paralleled by the exclusiveness of 'seed' and heredity within the covenant. This was to be steadily the burden of Paul's theology and it is important to take its measure fully. For Paul has sometimes been accused of making ill-considered attacks on mere legalism – the sort of legalistic attitudes which the best traditions in Jewry themselves disowned. He is thus liable to appear as discrediting an entire system on grounds which are thoroughly undeserved. The Pharisees were far from being the dull legalists that crude accusations suppose.

But this is to be crude also about Paul's anguish over the law. It was not simply that lawkeeping is tempted into fussiness about minutiae and a tyranny of the letter. It was the really basic problem of the law's failing to gain its ends by its means. Its means were commands, statutes, exhortations, covenants, precepts, and of course prohibitions, warnings, censures and retributions. Its ends were righteous dealing and integrity of soul. 'The end of the law' – that is, its goal and intention – was righteousness of life.

All too often, however, the 'end' of the law, in the other sense of 'end', was self-satisfaction, or incrimination; and so, in either case, defeat. It 'ended' in failure in that where it was broken it was bound to condemn. Condemnation, though logical and necessary, since without it the law would become a dead letter, was nevertheless also frustration. It merely registered that the law had *not* been fulfilled. Once done, that infringement could not be undone. The law 'required that which is past'. To condone would be to betray. But to indict, given the evil done, was also to forfeit the law's positive intention, and so to register its failure. This was the core of Paul's spiritual problem.

Even where the law 'succeeded' in being observed, a formal righteousness was always in danger of exciting self-congratulation, favourable comparison with law-breakers, and the lovelessness of the 'elder brother' in the parable. 'O God, I thank thee that I am not as . . .' When this happened law-keeping acquired an unworthiness which quite disqualified its external proprieties and turned its apparent recognition of God into an esteem of self. Then the motive of merit and public recognition of merit entered into its very probity and distorted all correctness of form. The law of itself seemed to offer no solution to these dilemmas of its own shaping. It could not abandon its due injunctions and prohibitions without betraying itself and also doing disservice to the human dignity and destiny which were its deepest significance. But equally it could not persist in its regulation of life without incurring these frustrations of righteousness which were present when sins occurred and penalties were demanded, or when observance, especially ritual observance, degenerated into pride and self-esteem.

No doubt the law could always await renewal in another place and time, could anticipate a future generation which would surmount these problems, or it could rely upon a 'remnant' – as the term went – which might escape them in a genuine sanctity. Yet the question remained whether the law did not somehow point beyond itself to a means for its ends free from these debilitating factors.

Our present concern, here, is with the significance of all this for universality, with the law's way of gravitating to exclusivism, not only from the side of covenant birth, but from the side of moral reprobation. Just as covenant and 'seed' must exclude the Gentile, so law-keeping tests must exclude the prostitute and the publican. When both categories of exclusion coincided, there was a powerful barrier indeed. When the second category occurred within the chosen 'seed' there was a powerful dilemma. That there were renegade Jews was, sadly, to be admitted, though the birth criterion was right. That there were Gentile yearners for a law of righteousness was, happily, to be recognised. Generous spirits in Israel rejoiced in godliness beyond their own borders. But however the paradox was to be understood – of godless 'seed' (*qua* behaviour) on the one hand and godly 'non-seed' on the other – the central issue remained: namely, that law in itself condemns what flouts it and what unworthily observes it, and that such condemnation draws the lines within society.

Before coming to Paul and Peter on this issue, it will be wise to pause and ask about the 'universalism' of Jesus which must surely have been the guiding factor in their debate. The great point to be made is that Jesus' welcome to the people of the law's failures within Jewry argues a welcome to the people lacking the birth criterion outside Jewry. For the twin categories of 'seed' and 'Sinai' belonged together. In other words, when Jesus overrode the moral frontiers of the law in welcoming Zacchaeus and Mary Magdalene, he foreshadowed how the same grace would override the ethnic frontiers in the inclusion of the gospel.

That he did not himself extend his ministry beyond the geographical boundaries of Palestine or – for the most part – beyond the social confines of 'the house of Israel', may be seen as a physical and historical necessity of that ministry itself. His purposive confinement does not argue a subsequent Jewish exclusivism in his Church or warrant the suspicion that apostolic 'gentilising' had betrayed his mind. On the contrary, the freedom with which the gospel of the kingdom in his hands transcended the law's scruples and hoped beyond the law's failures had latent in its grace the assurance which 'opened the kingdom . . . to all believers', irrespective of their past either of birth or of culpability. Whether ethnically or culpably excluded under law, humanity was neither ethnically nor culpably excluded from grace. If the Church obeyed an ethnic openness it was because Jesus had left the precedent in his readiness for rejects of the law's discipline of requirement and penalty.

There is, no doubt, a certain ambiguity in the Gospel sayings about a universal future. 'They shall come from the east, and from the west, and from the north, and from the south', says Luke 13:29, 'and shall sit down in the kingdom of God'. But was this solely from a Jewish dispersion? Matthew adds: 'with Abraham, and Isaac, and Jacob . . .' which some have taken to mean a non-Gentile mustering (8:11). But what, then, about the immediate contrast with 'the children of the kingdom cast out', if these new sharers are after all the ethnic 'seed'?

What are we to say, further, of the Gospels' indication that Jesus foresaw a universal future? 'Wheresoever this gospel shall be preached', he declared, 'throughout the whole world', the story of the woman who broke the alabaster box of ointment would be told 'for a memorial of her' (Matt. 26:13; Mark 14:9). How would she be known to the nations and not he? How would men tell the story of her anointing and not the meaning and mystery of his death for which her costly tribute was meant? Again, it is remotely possible to think of this 'story-telling' as confined to Jewish ears. But currency in the world can hardly be so confined, especially given the strong tradition that if 'the world' wants to know about Jewry it must come up to Jerusalem and enquire. Deliberate confinement of meaning does not go spreading leading stories across the lands.

When, according to the Fourth Gospel, enquiring Greeks came to Jerusalem (within the tradition just mentioned) 'to see Jesus', his indirect answer to them was that when he was 'lifted up' he would 'draw all men to' himself. This 'all' cannot mean a universally successful salvation, since the gospel never compels. It must mean a universally accessible salvation – a salvation to which men and women can be drawn without reference to prior conditions of race or culture or status. The clue to that accessible grace is said to be the Cross (John 12:32–33). It is only the suffering Messiah who can welcome all comers and his capacity to be the haven of their discordant diversity belongs with the love that redeems.

This is exactly what the great *Te Deum Laudamus* was to celebrate when it sang: 'When thou hadst overcome the sharpness of death thou didst open the kingdom of heaven to all believers'. To 'as many as received him', wrote the Fourth Evangelist, 'gave he power to become the sons of God, even to them that believe on his name . . . born not of blood, nor of the will of the flesh . . . but of God' (John 1:12–13). Here, clearly, the criterion of ethnic community has given way to that of faith-community. A new sort of peoplehood is in formation, requiring neither territory, nor statehood, nor heredity, for its cohesion and character, but only the criterion of faith. When later a Creed developed from and for this new people it spoke with a sublime, almost casual, simplicity of '. . . us men' – not 'us Jews and Gentiles', 'us blacks and whites', 'us cultured and uncouth'. For these inclusions are still making interior distinctions even in discounting them. 'Us humans' speaks a unity which has made all continuing disparities, for its purposes, quite irrelevant.

Neither Paul, nor Peter – certainly not Peter – had yet reached this clear conclusion. In conjecturing how they may have moved towards it we have to raise the question of time and date. Had Peter yet visited Cornelius? Very probably not. The chronology of Acts would seem to require Paul's visit prior to Peter's descent to Joppa. If not, then we have a clear index from Acts 10 of the firm line against Gentile inclusion in the gospel which Peter would have taken. If we *can* imagine Peter already in possession of the Cornelius experience then we know more surely the factors tending to the common mind, which the two apostles might have reached. So it will be truer to that future to let chronology be what it may and imagine Peter and Paul working out the significance of Cornelius together.

For Peter's role in the whole episode at Joppa has within it all the elements in the over-all decision – hostility, heart-searching, resistance, persuasion, conviction. To trace Peter's dramatic story will be to have all the features of Paul's parallel progress in more widespread travels and encounters. Such study will put us in the way of the ultimate conclusions, if not of the course of their actual debate during the fifteen days.

The Peter–Cornelius encounter is one of the most delightful incidents in the New Testament record. Peter, to start with, is away from Jerusalem, out from the citadel of privilege and its hard orthodoxy. He is down on the plain, eating humble pie with Simon a tanner. He is still strictly among 'disciples', Jewish believers. Around midday, he goes on to the flat roof to pray and after that to take lunch, and perhaps also to freshen with sea breezes the smelly air of the tanner's trade. There he fell into a doze and as he went off into a dream there were the vessels riding at anchor beyond the surf. This part of the Phoenician shore had no deep water harbour. Vessels unloaded on to lighters to get their merchandise ashore. So the last thing Peter saw as he mused were the coloured sails of the ships, dotting the skyline.

The coast right up to Tyre and to Sidon northwards was renowned for its far-flung commerce.

> Quinquireme of Nineveh from distant Ophir
> Rowing down to haven in sunny Palestine
> >   With a cargo of ivory
> >   And apes and peacocks,
> Sandalwood, cedarwood and sweet white wine.

The prophet Ezekiel has a glowing, if also imprecatory, description of the traffic of maritime Tyre in which, with their lesser renown, the Joppans also shared, reaching out certainly to their Phoenician cousins in Carthage and possibly even beyond the Pillars of Hercules to the western shores of Europe and Cornwall. Tyre, 'merchant of the people for many isles', made her ships from the oaks of Bashan, the cedars of Lebanon and the fir trees of Sinai. The 'fine linen with broidered work from Egypt' she spread forth to be her 'sail; blue and purple from the isles of Elishah' (Ezekiel 27:3–7). 'All the ships of the sea with their mariners' were in her 'to occupy her merchandise'. Arabia and the princes of Kedar were 'occupied' with her 'in lambs, and rams, and goats'. By these and many more, the Phoenicians were 'replenished and made very glorious in the midst of the seas' (Ezekiel 27:9, 21, 25) – all so different from the modest fishing smacks of Peter's Galilee.

So as he drowsed it seemed to Peter that the tall upright sails of fine Egyptian canvas were turned horizontal and let down before him like a spreading table-cloth. And of course they contained the cargoes transported in the holds and on the decks.

All Peter's unease at Gentile proximity in such impressive measure centred on the final taboo about common food. His one refuge was the dietary laws. These were the standing symbol of his Jewishness and the ultimate safeguard of identity. To break them would be the utmost in disloyalty and treachery. 'I will buy with you, sell with you, talk with you, walk with you . . . but I will not eat with you, drink with you, nor pray with you.' (Shylock in Shakespeare's *The Merchant of Venice*). Such was the unbreakable bond of his people, the essential securing of his Jewish being.

How shattering, even nightmarish, when the vision summoned him to 'kill and eat'. He felt nothing but revulsion at the sight of creeping things from foreign lands offered for his meal. 'Not so, Lord' was his emphatic response, escaping violently from the mere trace of compromise for having even heard such a bidding in his godly ears. 'Not so, Lord', he repeated with every fibre of his being and calling up all the faithful history of his personal integrity he insisted: 'I have never eaten anything common or unclean'.

Three times the hateful visual suggestion was repeated and each time Peter's rejection was answered with the puzzling formula: 'What God has cleansed you are not to consider unclean'.

On waking Peter was consumed with self-reproach at having seen and heard such defiling temptation and lost in a pained perplexity at what the vision could imply. Was he being plagued with damnable illusions or was he being grimly tested by perversions masquerading as divinely given?

Elucidation was near at hand. Three men, he was informed, were knocking at his door. They came, it transpired, at the command of another dreamer, one Cornelius, a Roman centurion from Italy, whose vision had given him explicit instructions to send for one Simon, address as supplied. Peter was resilient enough to entertain both them and their story, resolving cautiously to 'sleep on it', before deciding, equally cautiously, to go with them in the morning.

In the assembly that Cornelius had gathered to receive and hear him, Peter gained confidence. He was now in among the uncircumcised anyway and his Galilean ruggedness told him he had better see it through. The strange coincidence of the two dreams must have meaning. Shedding his fears, Peter told them all he knew, sharing with them the good news of Christ.

Reassuring evidence was soon to hand that the innovating Spirit had not deceived him. There was unmistakable faith and repentance in the response of his listeners. Peter was in no position to deny them the baptism they eagerly sought. Peter's loyalty to God had to concede development into what, by the old criteria, was thorough disloyalty but, by the new, the very mind and purpose of God. Not for the first time tradition had said 'No!' to God in mistaken zeal for God himself. Not for the first time was new obedience proved to be the only right form for past fidelity.

That Peter's conversion to the world was decisive became clear when, returning to Jerusalem, he was accused by still unliberated colleagues of unseemly conduct in entering a Gentile house. His response was simply to tell his story. His sufficient justification lay in the hand of God upon him and the plain activity of the Holy Spirit in the lives of these outsiders whom he had befriended. Paul seems later to have worried about Peter's dependability in this issue (Gal. 2:11). But then, Paul, too, had his reservations as is clear from the involved form of his argument about Jewish distinctiveness in Romans 9 to 11. In any event, his mood in Galatians is rigorous and combative. The once persecutor was not accustomed to a passionless logic.

The issue, manifestly, was a far-reaching one and subsequent counsels, described in Acts, cannot have been far from the thoughts of Paul and Peter in their meeting. What did the essential specialness of being Jewish really mean? How was it to be preserved if the Christian gospel was to be open impartially to all? Was such openness to be conditional on circumcision and the keeping of the Jewish Law? Could Gentiles be admissible to faith in Christ only if they first became Jews? Even that, for diehards, would have been a large concession. Or, more radically, were they acceptable simply on the ground of faith and repentance? If so, what became of the law as a whole? Its moral precepts had always been understood as requiring its ritual forms. If the entire Levitical code was to be seen as dispensable to Messianic acknowledgement, would the whole of society be thrown into permissiveness?

Was faith in Christ to imply a licence to the libertine? Were the pearls of Messianic joy to be cast to the swine of Gentile birth and manners? Could the gospel somehow be trusted to ensure that character and behaviour became consonant with faith? Even if so, how was the Jew in Christ to regard his current allegiance to Moses? How, indeed, was he to recognise himself in the new future?

It is difficult, in retrospect, to appreciate the torment of these questions for minds like Paul's and Peter's. But unless we do so, we fail in turn to appreciate how immense was the revolution which constituted the Church in Christ. The contrast between Jew and Gentile was – and remains – the most stubborn of all disparities within humanity. It is not simply that all identities are tenacious of themselves, that negroes know they are not whites, that Frenchmen stoutly refuse to be Turks, etc. Nor yet that all such consciousness of identity is sanctioned by language, race, territory, culture and tradition – those great constituents of all societies in the sense of themselves.

Jewry was all that – with the given land, the sacred language, the historical memory, the folk heroes, the ethnic stream and the distinctive tradition. But it was more. For these denominators of any society were all of them sanctioned, for Jewry, by a theology, a divine choice, so that the 'seed' was not just a physical ancestry but a 'chosen people', the Exodus not simply a historic migration but a heavenly design. The entry into the land had not been a bare tribal invasion but the assumption of a sacred destiny. It needs an effort of imagination for the modern Christian to realise how tenacious the resulting apartness and how radical, therefore, the initiative which surmounted it.

In some measure, we are disqualified from such realisation because of our very loyalty to what we call the Old Testament. We are still liable to see the continuing ethnic-religious particularity of Jewry as if it were not transcended by inclusion in Christ. We remain in divided mind, confessing that 'in Christ there is neither Jew nor Greek', and still assuming that the distinction yet obtains. Prevail it does, outside of Christ. No one disputes, or properly should want to dispute, the interior right of Jewish consciousness to believe itself in unique relation with God and God in unique relation with it. For such liberty of interior conviction is part of the due reverence in which all mystery must be held. But on Christian ground there is a single, no longer differentiated, access to grace and membership in Christ where all, irrespective of their antecedent histories, stand in utter equality of need and of love within the gospel of Christ. If we continue to use Hebrew psalms and draw inspiration from biblical history it must be in genuine loyalty to that uncompromising view of humanity as one in grace.

This was the deep trauma of persuasion through which Paul and Peter had to pass. They were helped, no doubt, by the rich tradition of universalism which belonged with their heritage from prophet and psalmist. The 'Old Testament' had a powerful sense of destiny towards all mankind and responsibility also. 'Look unto me, and be ye saved, all the ends of the earth' (Isaiah 45:22); 'the isles shall wait for his law' (Isaiah 42:4); 'He shall have dominion also from sea to sea' (Psalm 72:8); 'All nations . . . shall come and worship before thee, O Lord; and shall glorify thy name' (Psalm 86:9).

But there were two factors tending always to neutralise that universal view – factors which it was the task of the New Testament Church to overcome. The one was the constant failure of nerve, when the crunch came, really to admit those equal dimensions with all mankind. There was a recurrent loss of resolve and Israel drew back from genuine readiness for Gentile relationships. It did so for reasons which seemed valid in its own eyes – reasons which bring us to the second factor.

This was that universality, anyway, paradoxically demanded that it should not be complete. Else how was the instrumentality that pointed to it to be ensured? The nations must come to God *via* Israel. The situation might be loosely compared to that of democracy needing to withhold its own cherished freedoms from those suspected of coveting them for its very overthrow. Jewish exceptionality must go on as the necessary condition of the world's knowing the God of all the kindreds of men. Not for the first time in history was an agency holding on to a privilege as a condition of transcending it.

There could well be Gentilising, as it were, of God's compassions, but the special status need not, should not, be included. Or, if wisdom has pitched its tent in Israel (Wisdom of Solomon 10 and 11), then the would-be wise must seek it there. It might certainly be accessible to all so long as it also remained firmly with its copyrighted holders.

What the gospel of grace in Christ was doing was to make the universality total both as to content and as to instrument. The copyright, so to speak, passed into the public domain. All could now participate in its trusteeship as well as in its benediction, in giving it as well as in receiving it. This was the significance of the Church, as a community of faith and of obligation to the world. It did not turn upon ancestry, or upon territory, or upon ethnic covenant. It was constituted by faith, in openness to all lands, nations and cultures. When, over the century or so after the apostles, the Church became a largely Gentile reality by the self-exemption of Jewry, that exemption confirmed the insistent privacy with God that characterised Old Testament peoplehood even in its most open temper.

Paul and Peter did not have to cope with that trend of events and would certainly have deplored it. They were at the threshold of the problem of universality while the Church was still predominantly, and for some essentially, a Jewish thing. All that they could have discussed together lay on the nearer side of the great achievement of an open faith.

Peter later wrote to the 'strangers scattered throughout Pontus' and other provinces of Asia Minor and the Black Sea littoral (1 Peter 1:1). They could have been – some of them – 'strangers' in a Jewish dispersion. But some were certainly non-Jews. For he tells them (2:10) that 'in time past' they were 'not a people, but are now the people of God', clearly reflecting Hosea's distinction between 'seed-peoplehood' and 'true peoplehood' in heart. Is not this the same fascinating double meaning which we earlier noted in the teaching of Jesus about faith in unlikely places and failure in likely ones? Perhaps Peter wanted to keep the creative tension at this point between the ethnic and the spiritual criteria of community, the old and the new. For, if outsiders were now to be included, it did not mean that insiders were excluded. Grace was consistent and even-handed, within the simple condition of faith. Perhaps there were times when it was wise to let the ambiguity stand, lest ancient privilege should become resentful or new equality insensitive to history.

If so, Paul's temperament demanded the sharp focus of explicitness. We do not know how far his Arabian sojourn had been occupied with this question. It seems fair to suppose that the full definition of his position was subsequent to his time with Peter. Peter, as far as narrative reports, had had his first 'Gentile' baptism (if we may so speak) in the Cornelius episode. Paul's was by a prolonged encounter, in a wide dispersion, with the Jewish question. As befits the practical Galilean, Peter's conversion was in the simple terms of the episode at Joppa, where the many residual questions were left to the future and to the theorists. For Paul, however, these became central and mentally strenuous in a way they do not appear to have been for Peter.

To be sure, he had the same evident experience of Gentiles demonstrating 'repentance unto life'. Like Peter, he knew the reality of the fact of faith and its results in Gentile lives. But he also knew the strong counter-attack of Jewish status and Sinaitic privilege. The Judaisers, inside and outside the Church, dogged his way everywhere. He 'turned to the Gentiles', as he put it, in far more taxing terms than Peter's cor-

69

dial reception by Cornelius. Embarrassing as that had been for Peter, Paul shouldered the much more agonising tasks of disqualifying circumcision as a pre-requisite to Christ, of shepherding neophyte Christians to godliness without the constraints of Mosaic ritual, of developing a theology of law and grace which reconciled the ends of the former by the means of the latter, of asserting and ensuring liberty in Christ throughout his churches.

So it was that, precisely in a missionary context, he became the protagonist of the new faith within the old matrix. 'In Christ Jesus neither circumcision availeth any thing, nor uncircumcision, but a new creature' (Gal. 6:15). When he asked himself; 'What advantage then hath the Jew?' (Romans 3:1), he answered, that of historical vocation, the trusteeship of the oracles of God, the preparation for the realised Christ. This would always be the glory of Jewry without exceptionalising Jewry's position in the new order in other than historical terms. Theirs were the covenants and theirs the promises and theirs the context in which the worldwideness of salvation had originated.

There were times when Paul's Rabbinic training brought a certain subtlety into his logic, as he tried desperately to hold on to Jewish status and yet articulate unmistakably the inclusiveness of Christ. The issue about status, in his thinking, necessarily merged into that of the law. What had it served – that venerable heritage from Sinai? Clearly 'following after' the law of righteousness had not attained it (Romans 9:31) – not, that is, by the deeds the law prescribed or proscribed. For such deeds were inevitably wanting in fact, or wanting in worth, or both. Yet the summons to them was the divine tribute to the very dignity of man. The failure of the law within the law's people must be read as an education into grace. This grace would demonstrate the fidelity of the Lord from whom the law derived and achieve the fulfilment of the humanity for whom the law was meant.

'The law', Paul boldly declared, 'was our schoolmaster to bring us unto Christ' (Gal. 3:24). It ensured that we did not play truant from our true humanness as chartered by divine authority. It ensured that we were brought, firmly and squarely, to the place where evil would be both fully known and fully met.

Grace being its due goal and fulfilment, the law was satisfied in the work of faith. The exceptional privilege which its custody had rightly conferred would, therefore, pass into the new privilege and vocation of belonging with all mankind. So Paul, hammering out the meaning of his faith on the anvil of his faithfulness. The gospel, venerating its ethnic and historic roots, could not be other than universal. The Church, grateful for its spiritual ancestry, could not be other than physically heterogeneous. 'Whosoever will may come.' The heterogeneous church, we might say, was homogeneous only by virtue of men and women being in Christ.

How far that spiritual conclusion was advanced in Paul's thinking at the time of his fifteen days in Jerusalem is impossible to say, or how Peter's more prosaic mind or instinctive conservatism responded to him. What matters rather than the sequence in their convictions is their finality, whenever it was reached. But we may reasonably expect that they did converse together about the meaning of realised Messiahship for their understanding of worship.

Paul was later to use a graphic expression to describe his preaching ministry. He said that in his evangelism he was 'ministering the gospel' in order that 'the offering up of the Gentiles might be made acceptable'. The language he uses is liturgical. He sees himself as a priest in being a pastor and his 'priestly presentation' is that of the people whom he brings to faith. It cannot be that he is 'presenting' them against their will. Rather, their consent to faith involves them in the same 'presentation of themselves a living sacrifice' as that of all Christians (Romans 15:16, cp. 12:1). Bringing together twin aspects of ministry, which much Christian thinking has been prone to keep apart, Paul here ties a universal faith to a shared theology and a theology that means entire and personal doxology.

The open gospel in the open world certainly risked a diverse theology. That is exactly what Paul's detractors said. These ready admissions of 'believing' heathen into the faith-community would obviously jeopardise its purity of wor-

71

ship. These baptizands would bring their plural ideas, their deification traditions, their pantheon instincts, into the worship of their new confession. As a result, the holy unity of the God of Israel could well be forfeit. Paul's answer was that his ministering of the gospel was the surest antidote and that the gospel had within its very nature the power to refine the minds that responded to it.

That conversion must be in the mind as well as in the emotions, in the habit of thought as well as in the will, Paul knew from his own reflection. That it was so was part of the meaning of the Holy Spirit interpreting the Christ.

Was it in this context that Paul questioned Peter about Pentecost – that strange miracle of the tongues of fire and the fervent words intelligible to all language-groups in the crowded audience? Admittedly it was a Jewish assembly, exiles of the dispersion, with the common denominator of Moses and the Torah. So it was not yet the universal humanity that was to come. Nevertheless, the preaching of Peter had been taken into active comprehension, despite the Galilean accent, by all the auditors. Had this been meant as an active parable of the fact that the faith could, and should, 'go' into every language, and 'go' not merely in the geographical sense of travel but in the primary sense of intimate register within the soul? Whatever else may have been incidental to that birthday of the Church, this was its essential meaning. The event, which he had only by hearsay, gave Paul a clue in future problems when his own churches seemed to reproduce the ecstasy and the tongues. For, on that first occasion, what had mattered beyond all the exuberance and the astonishment, had been the solid, forthright, from-the-shoulder, speaking of Peter about crucifixion, resurrection, penitence, faith, baptism and witness. Paul's pastoral activity never lost sight of Pentecost as Peter's recollection told it.

But, relying on the gospel's power, in the Holy Spirit, to inform and discipline the converting mind, what of the worship to which its evangelical discipline would lead? We will turn to this question in the final chapter.

Here, in summary of these three chapters (2, 3 and 4), in the over-all theme of Peter and Paul and Jesus, let us prepare that final area of their conversation by isolating two vivid words from Matthew's account of the Cross. 'Sitting down, they watched him there . . .' (27:36). 'Him – there': the person and the place, Jesus and Golgotha. All the prelude of ministry out of which the passion had emerged is there in the identity. The sufferer is the teacher-healer. Without that history there would be no context for his suffering. Suffering, he did not cease to teach and heal: rather he taught more eloquently and healed more inclusively than ever. So all the earlier Jesus-story, the gospel *of* Jesus, is there inseparable from that climax.

From that climax begins to flow the gospel about Jesus. The Cross, in the light of resurrection, is seen as the answer, out of the wisdom and the power of God, to the evil of the world. That wisdom and power are present in the deliberate choices of Jesus – choices which he makes because he is party to the divine mind – which we call his Sonship to the Father. That divine action is visibly at grips with a situation which we can readily recognise as having within itself all the elements of human enmity to good, to love, to God. This enmity, characteristic of us all, is met and countered in the love that suffers. This love is of 'God . . . reconciling the world unto himself' (2 Cor. 5:19).

That Cross, with 'him there', has a physical, poetic gesture of embrace, resembling the human form in the act and in the art of love's appeal. Those arms, of the Cross, from the Cross, point round the world in a circle which meets around the whole. The price of that embrace is the Cross itself. For embrace is the contradiction of immunity. One cannot love without risk. What Paul later called 'the marks of Jesus' (Gal. 6:17) are the wounds of love.

All this is the meaning of 'him there' – this person, this place. Together they constitute where God is and where, by being there 'in Christ', God is known for who he is. It is here that Christian theology finds its distinctive truth – a truth which quite radically transforms – yet also fulfils – the past of the Bible's theology. How it does so we must now take up.

The seventeenth-century poet Richard Crashaw, in *Charitas Nimia* (or *The Dear Bargain*) asks the question:

> Lord, what is man? why should he cost thee
> So dear? what had his ruin lost thee?

Heaven, he argues, would heaven be, though mankind should dwell in lowest hell. 'What have his woes to do with thee?' Cherubim and seraphim would still sing: 'Holy, holy, holy'. Angels would not cease their unresting praise. Heaven is surely serene in a sublime indifference to man?

> Let froward dust then do its kind;
> And give itself for sport to the proud wind.
> Why should a piece of peevish clay plead shares
> In the Eternity of thy old cares?
> Why should'st thou bow thy awful breast to see
> What mine own madnesses have done with me?

Crashaw's final question is:

> If I were lost in misery,
> What was it to thy heav'n and thee?

The Christian answer, because of Christ, is 'everything'. We believe unashamedly in the God with wounds, because we believe consistently in the God with seraphim and majesty. He is more convincingly in heaven for having come from it – a conviction on our part which is altogether consistent with what we believe about creation, about Sinai, about prophets. But it is all evident for us in the man from Galilee, the master carpenter of Nazareth 'who on the Cross through wood and nails' has fashioned man's salvation.

Thanks to 'him there' we now have the ultimate criterion of omnipotence and the final perspectives for theology. Let us trace this confidence back to our two apostles.

Study Points and Questions
   (1) 'The gospel by its very nature has to be universal.' How would you explain this 'necessity'?
   (2) How would you relate this apostolic obligation to universality and the undoubted geographical confinement

of Jesus' own ministry?

(3) What would be your response to the question : Did Jesus intend the Church?

(4) 'I, if I be lifted up, will draw all men unto me' (John 12:32). Not, we said, a universally successful salvation, but a universally accessible one. Why is the Cross a universally relevant reality? In what sense was Jesus' comment an answer to the Greeks who in John 12 came 'seeking' him?

(5) If the gospel was inherently universal why was it that the first apostles had such reluctance to let it be so? How were their legitimate misgivings met and their improper hesitations overcome?

(6) Peoplehood to God, we say, is thrown open to all by the New Testament. How would you react to the claim of some Jewish thinking that, even so, the Church is just another form of exclusivism because it puts right belief where the old covenant had right birth. Humanity can only be 'God's people' by satisfying right conditions. So the universalism is really phoney. Belief, too, is very often the 'accident' of birth. So is the New Testament less than honest about its 'privacy' and not at all truly open?

(7) How do you understand the significant comment of Paul in Romans 15:16?

(8) Peter learned at Joppa that old loyalties have sometimes to give way to new ones. Have you known this experience? Is the Church at any Joppa juncture now?

(9) 'Being hospitable in the hospitality of God.' What would you say of this as a definition of the ministry of the Church? How do we fulfil it?

5: The Name of the Lord at Jerusalem

Authority and experience, corporate tradition and personal charisma, history and faith, the cross and theology, grace and mission, Jew and Gentile – all these, we may be sure, were themes of the rendezvous of Paul with Peter, their days and nights of conversation. Immersed in them so intensely, they could hardly have failed to talk about Jerusalem. Awareness of the Holy City must have laid its impress upon every other topic. Herod's splendid temple dominated the skyline and the Upper Room of the first Eucharist and of Pentecost stood, we may surmise, on the very hill of Zion. For the Galilean Peter, Jerusalem was the great metropolis which every provincial held in awe. For Paul it was redolent with his Rabbinic discipline, his religious nurture at the feet of Gamaliel. For both it was the place where Jesus had been crucified: the site of Calvary lay only a stone's throw from the western wall. By its unique character it brought together the situation-theology in which the faith and the Church together were born. For the event of the Cross and the Resurrection had occurred precisely where, as the old prophet had it, God had chosen to set his Name. We can, then, covet in imagination to overhear the two apostles in mutual exploration of the sacrament of geography so dear to every Jewish heart in the fair – now darkly tragic – place where 'the tribes go up ... to give thanks unto the name of the Lord' (Ps. 122:4).

'The place and the name', from the time of David, had always been intimately one – *Yad va Shem*, as the Hebrew is. In Israeli Jerusalem today that title belongs to the gaunt memorial to the victims of the Holocaust which stands close to the Herzl National Park on the western edges of the modern city. Its conception fulfils the founder's dream in which he saw an endless procession of people, filing one by one into death, the six million Jews of Hitler's prolonged pursuit of genocide. He determined that all those nameless victims would find 'a place and a name' in the rebirth of the Jewish State and on the very soil of David's city of peace.

The interior of the Yad Vashem Memorial commemorates, in oppressive concrete-shrouded gloom, lit only by the steady flame of remembrance, the several locations of the death camps – Belsen, Auschwitz, Dachau and the rest. Charred wood and iron bars, barbed wire and an incineration chimney, symbolise the unnameable horrors, beyond which the passion of achieved survival celebrates an inextinguishable hope, while the anguish of non-survival, non-rescue, non-pity, non-compassion, remains the ever present burden of the Israeli soul. For there is a tormenting sense, as Elie Wiesel expressed it, that 'at Auschwitz not only man died but also the idea of man' (in *Legends of Our Time,* p. 190). So Yad Vashem is, for all Israelis, the focus of their most agonising debate, how to live within, and yet beyond, the past, how to reconcile memory and hope. Theology, some hold, can never be the same after the Holocaust. Jerusalem has to reckon with the most ultimate negation of 'the name of the place', with an overwhelming trauma of 'the absence of God'.

It is well to begin in this way with the passionate perplexity, shrined in modern Jerusalem and calling into question the most ultimate dimensions of theology's assumption of God. To some Jerusalem thinking, all Christian confidence in the Jesus-lovingness of God (if we may so phrase it) is obsolete because it is pre-Holocaust. What happened at Calvary, as Christians have seen and said it, can no longer be the decisive event in salvation-history because it can no longer be the focus of an ultimate evil matched by heavenly love. In Jewish immolation by Hitler there is a measure of Godforsakenness which goes far beyond the Cross and in which there was no resurrection – other than that of a remnant by their own resources. 'The Godforsakenness of Jesus', writes Roy Eckardt, 'has become non-absolute, if it ever was absolute'.

This radical interrogation of our faith, voiced from Jerusalem itself in this late twentieth century, is one to which our sense of 'God in Christ' must be ever open. The gospel never suggested that there was something quantitatively unique about the suffering of Jesus. The faith, rather, has been that in the will to crucify, to immolate the Sermon on the Mount in the person of the preacher, we can find a register of the tragedy of our humanity. Enormities in history, and the Holocaust supremely, but not alone among them, exceed it infinitely in incidence and range. But this need not disqualify the measure it affords us of those human sins which, when corroborated and further suborned by the enmities of nations and the corruptions of absolute power, will exterminate and liquidate – with reckless repudiation both of God and man. Elie Wiesel's most eloquent writing on the Holocaust is *Night*. At the dying of Jesus, there was 'darkness over all the land'.

Saul and Simon looked back on the martial travail of the Maccabees, those Jewish heroes of resistance. But in their own context, Judaism was a *religio licita* and their complaints of Rome were not about annihilation. In the very near Christian future persecution lay ahead and was to claim them both for martyrdom. At the moment of their historic meeting their pre-occupation with the mystery of suffering and death was a pre-occupation with the meaning these had had for and in Jesus. Their mental and spiritual pre-occupation was 'him there', with the substance of their counsels the themes we have tried to estimate. How, from those several areas of anguish and conviction of mind, did their theology begin to find its way towards the central Christian assurance of love as the wisdom in divine power? In short, what, in Jesus, was the Name chosen to 'dwell in the place' – the place where the Name was to be known? How did they, how do we, move from 'him there', Jesus, Lord and Saviour, to 'God here' – here in this place of his disclosure of his Name?

Only tragically. Revelatory history has happened in that tragic history enshrines it. This has always been so. We have noted that 'the prophets' could not be fulfilled in words alone. And the tragic histories matter, even for the reproach in them, if only because we do not suppose a divine indifference. Sceptics do not always see this. They complain about evils and accuse divine responsibility for them, and then conclude divine non-existence or unreality. But by that conclusion evil too evaporates into something we cannot reproach. Indeed, one of the surest evidences for the divine reality is the very passion we feel about what is wrong – a passion which assumes there *is* an ultimately liable power responsibly involved. If that is not the case, 'evils' may occur as events we suffer, but they cannot occur as wrongs we accuse. Conversely, we could ignore historical tragedy if we were to believe in some transcendent serenity indifferent to any and every history and celestially oblivious of man. Such philosophic immunity of the divine, such irrelevance of divinity, is not the biblical way. God, as the Bible understands, is committed in and to history. Theology is always situation-taught, because revelation is eventful and event is revelatory.

Jerusalem, by biblical consensus, is the city which gathers to itself the sacramental quality of time and space because it focusses the land as a whole and the land, in turn, is the arena of divine purposes, the ground of divine action. Its capture from the Jebusites under David and its establishment as the capital unified the northern and the southern enclaves of post-Exodus Jewry, welding both Samaria and Hebron into a single monarchy in a status which has always survived the political ruptures which so quickly ensued.

The centralisation of worship, achieved in Solomon's temple, gave an experience of unity which no experience of exile could altogether extinguish. It also provided a physical disqualification of all those local nature worships or private divinities to which religious sentiment was so often prone. Jerusalem thus became at once the sentinel and the citadel of an undivided worship, the sanctuary of the Name of the Lord, 'who dwelleth in Zion'.

Yet it was also the sign of a privacy of its own. Its possession of, and by, Jewishness gave an intensity to its character such as Athens or Alexandria never matched. It was 'thither the tribes' went up – 'the tribes of the Lord'. The house of God had only a courtyard for the Gentiles and such might not pass beyond those outer precincts. There is nothing in all religion more potent than the paradox of inclusion on exclusive terms, and this Jerusalem completely represented. It possessed the fascination both of monopoly and universality. Peter, out of Galilee, and Paul out of Tarsus, were sons of that tension and their presence in its very haunts meant that it came searchingly into their exchanges.

But their concern with history and locale, as we have seen, was more immediate than the significance of David's king-ship and Solomon's temple. The place of the city and the Name of the Lord had now to be read by the clue of the recent events of Jesus' death and resurrection, and their genesis of the believing community. These were one with the biblical precedent of historical revelation. By that precedent Peter and Paul were to be pioneers in identifying as the finally decisive historical reference for God the fact of Jesus' Cross. For them Good Friday, with its sequel, was seen to be the day on which, in line with Isaiah 25:9, they could say: 'Lo, this is our God; we have waited for him . . . this is the Lord; we have waited for him, we will be glad and rejoice in his salva-tion'.

The instinct to find God in the historical and to know the historical 'finding' them, as authentic of God, was the same, on their part, as the long Hebraic tradition. The difference lay in moving on from Exodus and Exile, from emancipations via the Red Sea and Jordan, and from liberation under Cyrus, to the Christ-Passover (as Paul was later to call it) and to the constitution of the people of God in 'the body of Christ'.

The literal 'him there' which we cited in closing chapter 4, became for them, not simply a factual truth of the con-demned teacher, but the central person-point of Messiahship; and so, in ultimate meaning, the essential disclosure of the God behind Messiahship. There at the Cross was the place where the Name had been made to belong. Jerusalem's final meaning, as the sacrament-point of God in history, had been realised in 'God in Christ'. Paul and Peter conversed under its very shadow and found it the very shade of the divine hand.

We can explore this further if we look at a precedent in Exodus 3, where event and disclosure coincided in the experience of Moses. The bush that burned with fire arrested the shepherd-prince and the voice out of the bush summoned him to lead his slave people into liberty. Keenly aware of their mob mentality, their fickleness and fear, he nervously asked for some guarantee that the summons was genuine and the project viable. He imagined himself in turn summoning his people and being interrogated by them as to his credentials, which effectively meant God's credentials. What was he to say? 'What is his name?' 'What shall I say to them?'

The familiar response, 'I am that I am' seems at first a mocking answer. How is a philosophic enigma any response to an urgent, existential, question? One does not hearten slaves with verbal puzzles. Nor should one equivocate about serious and risky destiny.

Rightly read, however, the reply does not equivocate. Nor does it deceive. It should be read: 'I will be there as he who I there will be'. The guarantee is in the divine character. But in the nature of things one cannot experience it in advance. There cannot be antecedent certainties; only a readiness to trust. It is in Exodus alone that the God of Exodus is known. 'I will be there as he who I there will be.' Once the event has been lived, then its import is known. Theology or, better, experience, can then turn the significance into the past tense, into stated experience which then reassures every new present. The Exodus is then an Ebenezer. 'He has been there as he who he there has been.' God, in other words, sets his clue within history. Such con-clue-sion, if we can venture the term, is precisely what constitutes Old Testament conviction. 'All our fathers were under the cloud, and all passed through the sea' (1 Cor. 10:1). He led them out that he might bring them in . . . (Deut. 4:37–38).

It is this same instinct for history as housing through experience the authentic knowledge of God which the early Church followed, taught by its Judaic training. That instinct belongs with the entire Bible. But the definitive event is radically new. It was no less than revolutionary to identify, in Christ crucified, the power and the wisdom of God. That 'God was in Christ, reconciling the world unto himself' was to be the very heart of the Petrine/Pauline gospel.

It was this instinct which made the New Testament. As we have seen, the four Gospels insistently tie back everything to a Jesus-history and in telling that history they find a dominating climax in suffering and death. The Gospels are all 'passion narratives with extended introduction'. The prelude is important and has to do with teaching and character. But it leads directly into the crowning dimension. There is between teaching and suffering, between ministry and rejection, a single thread of revelation both in word and deed.

Thus the very nature of the Gospels as documents and as literature shows how inferential history defines Christian faith and how faith is essentially a history-telling thing. Faith is not an abstraction of vision, a flight of philosophic fancy, a plunge into the unknown. It stands in the 'him there' situation, where a person and a place combine into a conviction believed to be conclusive about God. 'He has been there as he who he there has been.' This, for Paul as for Peter, is the *who* and the *where* of divine identity. Here is the everywhere of God.

Did Paul and Peter concelebrate the Eucharist during their fortnight of conversation? Paul insists in Galatians that he did not consult more widely than with Peter. But this need not mean that he was otherwise in complete isolation. Acts certainly suggests that 'he was with them coming in and going out'. It could hardly be that the two apostles had no sacramental fellowship as the setting of their mutual theology.

Peter's tragically intimate knowledge of 'the same night in which he was betrayed' and Paul's ignorance of it could find a present unity in re-enacting the event in the bread and the wine. For the Lord's Supper has commemoratively just that same retrospect which the Gospels have historically and it re-creates the continuing fellowship by which the faith is told. It sets a new peoplehood in the sequel to a new exodus. On every count, then, whether of document or sacrament, the New Testament renews, with a Jesus perspective, the biblical confidence that event is revelation. Experience has brought us to the God of salvation through the salvation of God.

We can reverently overhear Peter and Paul talking of 'the exodus' Jesus had accomplished in Jerusalem, anticipating the theology of their epistles and their ministry. 'The God of all grace' (1 Peter 5:10); 'the God of patience' (Romans 15:5);

'the God of hope' (Romans 15:13); 'the God of peace' (Romans 15:33) were among the descriptives they subsequently used. What a divine characterisation they affirm, once we measure this grace, this patience, this hope, this peace, in terms definable by reference to Jesus and the Cross! They are the elaboration in Christian sense of 'the Name of the Lord', known at Jerusalem.

We have seen in chapter 4 what it meant to understand 'the God of all grace' from the Christhood of Jesus. We know 'the love of God . . . in Christ Jesus our Lord', and how God 'commendeth' it to us 'in that, while we were yet sinners, Christ died for us' (Romans 5:8). 'Commending' means that God attests what his love is by this measure and urges upon us the realisation of it. He signifies to us in Jesus as the Christ the criterion by which he would be known. Peter, in his personal way, tells us the same truth, describing his scattered flock as those who 'by him' (i.e. by Jesus – the Jesus of the Cross) have believed in God so that their 'faith and hope might be in God' (1 Peter 1:21). The ground of all his pastoral care for purity, for long-suffering and for fellowship is in the significance of the one 'who his own self bare our sins in his own body (up to) the tree' in order that we might 'live unto righteousness' (1 Peter 2:24).

To understand in this way 'the place of the Name of the Lord' is to share the Christian theological decision which the New Testament enshrines. 'The love of Christ', says Paul, 'decides us'. His word in 2 Corinthians 5:14 ('constraineth' in the AV) means quite literally 'makes up our mind' by leaving us no other option save a reverent acknowledgement. The metaphor of the verb he uses is of one who cannot escape or elude the logic of a situation. Here, spiritually discerned, is the altogether persuasive thing, able to outweigh all those dissuasions as to God which belong with our human experience of despair, or confusion, or evil and self-reproach. Circumstances which argue all these persist and dog our path. But they are containable within the counter-assurance that avails for us in Christ. From that reality they have no final power to isolate or bar us. This Christ-logic justifies the confidence that *nothing* 'shall be able to separate us from the love of God . . . in Christ Jesus our Lord' (Romans 8:39).

To think this Christ-criterion of God the climax of the Peter/Paul conversation is only to anticipate what the New Testament became. For ourselves, and for all theists, such as our two apostles already were, it is vital to realise what a large development it meant in theological conviction. To do so we need to raise for ourselves some fundamental questions of theology, whether or not we can assume that Paul and Peter talked of them in quite the way we must. There was, in their day, no historical Islam to underline the issues in the form which Islamic monotheism does.

Nor did Paul, for all his travail about Torah and Israel, possess the perspective on Judaism which must be ours these centuries on. For Judaism, through those centuries, has continued in steadfast, often heroic, dissociation from – indeed sharp disavowal of – the Christian understanding of 'God in Christ'. The significance of that faith in a single 'Testament', neither 'old' nor 'new', must be for us a positive reality.

The theology of divine unity which is common to the three Semitic theisms will be the right frame of reference in which to explore the distinctively Christian measure of the One Lord. We moderns can never precisely know what apostles would have done in our situation. But that need not prevent us from studying their, now ancient, then new-found, thrill of faith in a context that is ours. Nothing exhaustive can be attempted here; only some thoughts on 'God in Christ' from the angle of God as One in other faiths.

Any faith in God entails faith in divine involvement with mankind. The question between us, Jews, Muslims and Christians, is the degree of that engagement with the human scene. None of us worship a divine absentee, an eternal unconcern. On such terms the word 'God' would be empty of all meaning. It is in relevance to us that God is known. What relevance is the question. The word 'God', like the word 'friend', is a relational word: it has to do with what is between two parties. God, as the Danish thinker, Kierkegaard put it, 'is never the third party'. He is always the One 'with whom we have to do' (Hebrews 4:13) and his reality is experienced in relationship, not in abstraction. Divine reality outside such relationship is also outside meaning and so is no part of theology.

This is not to say that the divine reality is exhausted in the human relationship or that relevance to ourselves is the only measure of our worship. Quite the contrary. Theology, in all the monotheisms, has always been careful to ponder what has been called 'the hiddenness of God', the transcendence, the impenetrability which is 'dark with excess of light', the mystery which escapes or defies our comprehension.

In all theistic traditions there has been a strong 'negative theology', a *theologia apophatike,* as the Greeks called it, where western religion comes closest to Asia and to Hindu ideas. On this ground it is held that *all* human concepts in some sense 'betray' the reality of what is 'wholly Other'. Ideas, too, can be idols and must be confessed false. For God cannot possibly be 'represented' and if ideas are thought, as it were, to 'capture' him, they have to be renounced, being just as delusory as physical images themselves. On this count, the 'character' of God, if we may so speak, must remain altogether indefinable. All that a loyal theology could say, after saying anything, was: 'But God is *not* that'.

The force and persistence of these instincts to see God as being altogether beyond 'attribution' of 'character' on the part of our minds, are witness enough to what we may call the diffidence of theologians. But, except as a warning against superficial simplicity, they are quite incompatible with Christian faith.

Reflecting on 'negative theology', the Persian Muslim mystic Jalāl al-Dīn Rūmī asked:

Why this oft repeated Naught?

and replied:

Naught brings you first upon the track of aught.
Though idle air may seem the Negative
It wafts faint odours of the Positive.

But 'faint odours' are not 'God in Christ'. A Christian theol-

85

ogy, far from being sanguine, or unmindful of mystery, does make bold to believe that what in God transcends our knowing *is* consistent with what is within our knowing – consistent even though still transcending. In other words we do not believe that what is beyond our grasp cancels what is within it. We do not affirm and negate at the same time. To do so is futility. Theology is not a semantic game, a seeking of the hidden and a hiding of the sought. It is doxology – an adoring of the Lord, 'only and divinely like himself'.

There is something uniquely Christian about this faith that God is dependably known, that he may exceed our grasp but does not elude it. Yet this faith is, for us Christians, the logic of beliefs which we share very firmly with other theists – beliefs as to creation, revelation, prophethood and providence.

Take creation. Peter, in his First Epistle, minted the phrase 'a faithful Creator' (1 Peter 4:19). The adjective 'faithful' there gets just the point we are making, namely that God can be trusted to be consistently what the created order suggests he is. For creation, involved further, as it is, with revelation and prophethood as its chartering, means divine action arising from divine being. In the action, being is expressed. 'The heavens declare the glory of God; and the firmament sheweth his handiwork' (Ps. 19:1).

Some Judaic thinking was liable to put God's glory at one remove from God himself, just as the *shekinah,* or 'presence', could be dissociated, for reverence sake, from the divine essence. But these were instincts of theological coyness with which we can sympathise without conceding that there is any real distinction between God and his 'glory'. Only as these are inseparable can either be. Paul in his journeys among pagans and philosophers often used the theme of creation and of nature commending the grace of the 'God who commanded the light to shine out of darkness'.

The 'faithful Creator', as Peter and Paul believed, was such, because his faithfulness had issued into that relationship with human history which the gospel saw in Jesus Christ. Seeing Christ, it became clear to them for the first time what the word 'God' really meant. As R. G. Collingwood remarked:

> The thought of God as watching over the life of the world, directing the course of its history, judging its actions and bringing it back ultimately to unity with himself is a thought without which we can hardly think of God at all.

For only such thinking does justice to the sovereignty of God.

In the thought-exchanges of Peter and Paul, though we have no means of transcribing them verbally, this could not fail to be the crowning theme – 'God in Christ' as the ultimate confirmation of God in creation, God in the unity of shaping and saving the world, thereby dependably known as love, for love and in love.

Whether through fifteen days or nineteen centuries, such is still the apostolic theme. There are theologians, to be sure, who have depreciated the creation-faith in a desire to exclude from sole faith in Christ any rational reverence in the cosmos. But this misunderstands the nature of the Christ. Messiahship, as St John's Prologue underlines, is continuous with creation. It is the 'God who commanded the light to shine out of darkness (who has) shined in our hearts' (2 Cor. 4:6).

Let us try to follow further this apostolic thought of the power that is behind creation being one with the love that brings the Messiah. 'By the Christ the worlds were made' they said. To understand this we must see how nature itself is sacramental, how God entrusts nature to man as that in which he will find and fulfil his autonomy, his 'dominion'. We then further see how man, in spite of law and prophet for his guides, perverts that trust, and disorders his world. Then further yet, we see how God undertakes the salvation of that human tragedy. To realise how all these belong together is to understand the 'unity' of God: it is to 'have' the God of patience, hope and peace, of whom Paul and Peter talked and wrote. It is also to measure realistically and to be honest about the human situation as history shows it to be. On both counts, it is to see God and man in that relationship which is the clue to either.

Faith about 'creation', we should be clear, is not primarily about a 'when' and a start. It is about a 'why' and an intention. 'Beginning' is initiative. Doubtless, being human, we think time: time is needed to note a time; time at which implies time before which. That problem in any temporal 'start' is an accident of our way of thought. But 'creation' means the divine 'wantedness' of this world. It is a taking away of the nothingness, a bringing-to-be that fulfils a will that there should be.

'God said, Let there be . . . and there was . . .' (Gen. 1:3). Put negatively, the world is not a blunder, or a prank, or a fraud, or a mechanism, or a futility. It is a divinely wanted thing, necessary to God as art is to an artist, or music to a musician, so that his independence of it is not in doubt. By this analogy of authorship, we can see how God is *both* transcendent and involved, free and yet liable, beyond and yet for the world. He cannot create and be as if he had not. This engagement with men, however, is no external limitation. For it comes by and in his own willing. Creation, therefore, means that God has liabilities about man and man legitimately has claims on God. Being within the divine Creator's nature, this spells no compromise of his sovereignty. It is his sovereignty that wills it so.

This is what we mean when we affirm his unity. What we have in creation is a cosmos, not a chaos. As creatures willed to be, we do not worship sheer causality mechanically enthroned. We do not worship sheer omnipotence tyrannically inscrutable. We do not worship total aloofness callously serene, a deity whose greatness consists in withholding any dignity from us.

No! We worship a Creator, the Creator, a God great enough to set such high regard upon his creatures, a God who risks his purposes on their response; entrusts nature's order into their dominion, makes them tenants, farmers, polytechnocrats, within his world; artists, priests and poets, interpreting his universe. He made them for himself. He walks in the garden of creation calling for the creature. There is this genuine mutuality between ourselves and him. 'Adam, where art thou?' echoes our own awareness of a destiny in and unto him. So he is no final enigma, no absolute potentate, no eternal spectator.

On the contrary, he constitutes a *milieu divin,* where we live and move and have our being. Nature is the sacrament of that exchange. 'The creature is one with God in the very fact of being other than God.' God's heavenly otherness, or beyondness, where worship adores, is responsive to our otherness as creatures. It is an otherness meant for communion. The world is thus the sacramental ground of divine-human relationship.

It is just this which is confirmed by the reality of sin. One of the surest evidences of the divine is what happens in us when we deny or defy him. There is about man a restlessness which forbids him to rest in false absolutes which he has himself enthroned. For then he suffers from 'the wound of absence', willed absence, 'the wound of defiance' we might call it.

In the familiar words of Augustine's prayer: 'Thou hast made us for thyself and our hearts are restless till they rest in thee'. Some old philosophers, out of favour now, used to claim that thought contained the idea of that perfection which could not fail to exist. Therefore, exist it did. We would be sounder to restate that case, not on reason, but on the heart. For when the heart absents itself from God it finds that the absence disqualifies the heart. 'Thou hast set eternity in our hearts.'

But it is an eternity which a man may try to exclude. The love which, quite literally, 'fulfils' him, is only present by consent. On so many counts in our experience, we learn the deference God practises towards our responsibilities. But his patience is never indifference, nor is his purpose other than persistent.

That our relation to God is free to be one that rejects its proper partnership of love, so that it becomes instead an otherness of alienation and self-will, is the clear witness of the history of law and revelation. These, as we have seen, are clearly continuous with creation. Torah, as Paul and Peter knew it, was an invitation to respond, a charter of right humanness under God, of sacramental behaviour in nature, as family, sex, tribe, land and labour, wealth and health, took nature in their possessive stride. Such invitation met refusal. Moses himself descended from the Mount of the Law into the obscenity of the golden calf, shattering the tablets in an anger of despair. But he was summoned back to receive them again. The golden calf, though the human folly, was not the human truth. God does not weary of mankind; he is Paul's 'God of patience'.

So there is a steady reiteration of the invitation, through the steadfast ministry of the prophets. Just as law means that God does not leave creation unchartered, so prophethood means that he does not leave law unchampioned. Yet its very reiteration, though reassuring about divine fidelity, makes sombre reading in its verdict about man. It shows all too tragically how perverse he can become.

Whether or not in converse with Peter, Paul was to be the great apostolic explorer of this perversity in man, as the Epistle to the Romans makes plain. In this as in other aspects of his mental leadership, Paul has often been misunderstood and even maligned. We have seen earlier that he was not merely denouncing a legalistic spirit when he wrote about the Torah. His case was not merely that there are fastidious, meticulous literalists fussing over minutiae. He was raising the deep problem of the perverse will itself. Like Jesus himself in his teaching, Paul too was going back into the final motives, as distinct from the external acts. He was wrestling with the defectiveness of law, both when evil is committed and when good is corrupted by merit and congratulation. He was burdened to find some way beyond the falsehood in condoning and the negation in condemning. He saw that what could only be, by its nature, first hortatory and then retributive, would never meet the misery of man. What was he to do himself with a disordered will?

We must, with him, be endlessly thankful that law at least identifies our perversity for what it is. Otherwise, unconvicted and unshown to ourselves, we would be in worse case still. Law is thus the blessed diagnostician of our experience. It witnesses to the dignity and vocation of man. Its claim upon us is the deepest tribute to our stature, as meant for the discipline of God's society. But that end or goal remains unfulfilled.

Had Paul yet formulated his vigorous theology of sin when he talked with Peter? Was it hammered out on the anvil of their conversation? We cannot say. What is not in doubt is that for each of them Torah was the prelude to Christ. It ensured that men could neither evade nor deny the problem of themselves. It held before them an ideal which both ennobled and condemned them. It identified them both for what they were meant, and what they failed, to be. So it pointed them on to something beyond itself where both its meaning and its failure would be met.

If this tells us the law-to-Christ sequence from within the experience of human sin, how should we see the law-Christ sequence within the economy of divine action? It is here that we are back with the full New Testament implication of calling God 'a faithful Creator'. Its meaning is that – to put it colloquially – God 'comes through' with what is needed, consistently with his nature and loyally to his creation. What, when it happens, we know as 'Messianic', that is divine action about man, is so, and is such, because of who God is. The enterprise of Jesus as the Christ unfolds from within the divine nature as God's response to human creaturehood in its lostness. Were there no such enterprise – history being the wayward thing we tragically find it to be – then the Creator would not have kept faith with creation. The creative intention would have been thwarted by divine neglect or abandonment. Then, in a very real sense 'God' would no longer be God.

Here in *this* measure of divine liability 'for us men and for our salvation', we have the distinctively Christian dimension of theology. Other monotheisms travel only part of this distance with us, by their faith in creation and law.

To grasp it let us turn again to a great word in Paul, *kenosis*. He was later to make it central in one of his finest writings – Philippians 2. *Kenosis,* there and elsewhere, means the divine compassion's self-emptying. This metaphor of 'emptying' should not be misunderstood by reference to a material container. When a wine-bottle is 'emptied' the contents are no longer there. People have quaintly asked: 'If what makes God God is thus emptied, how does the event remain divine?' The meaning is not that sort of 'emptying'. Instead, it is close to the modern idea of status. Status is normally self-guarding, self-preserving, jealous that it should not be mistaken by being taken for less than it is. Master-carpenters will stage a strike if one is asked to do a labourer's job. (He may be thought no more than a navvy next time.) The colonel will not forget his rank and the private must salute it. Such is status whose being is to be acknowledged.

Many think of God in just these terms, Muslims most of all, but lots of Christians too. Divinity cannot afford to be mistaken for less than it is. We are jealous, like Elijah, for 'the Lord of hosts'. It is almost as if, at times, 'almightiness' is understood as sheer superiority. God is then altogether great only by keeping us helplessly small. Worship is then likely to be simply the prudence of sycophants.

But, truly, the Christian understanding of God is not this way. Such status-hunger is incompatible with love. The standing of God is more like that of a shepherd, or a father, where the very status is costly to the bearer, where there is a self-expenditure in the very nature of the case. There is a kind of status which consists in giving itself away, whose securities have no need of jealousies and where one-up-manship is never practised. Wherever love entails demands, love undertakes them and refuses to economise itself. This is just what Philippians 2 says about Christ and, because of Christ, about God in Christ. The Lord Jesus did not count divine status a treasure to preserve at all costs but 'took upon him the form of a servant', and 'humbled himself . . . even (to) the death of the cross'. In that loving self-giving the heart of God is self-revealed.

This is the Christian understanding of God. But it is important to see how it is continuous with, or the final measure of, what can be seen to be implicit in creation. For, there also, God limits sheer or overwhelming status-sovereignty in the course of an enterprise with and in man. Such limitation is within the true meaning of omnipotence. It is not externally imposed, implying some necessity which makes God less than ultimate. It is from within his own nature and in loyalty to liabilities for his own creation, love determining what those liabilities require.

Whether or not the Paul/Peter conversation in Jerusalem reached the phrasing of Philippians, who can say? But this was where Christian conviction was moving. The servant language central to Philippians had been made the clue to Messiahship, as argued in chapter 3, in the consciousness of Jesus himself, or, as some would prefer to say, in the conviction of the first Christians about how that consciousness had been. The servant in Isaiah 42 and 53 had been a sufferer through his fidelity as servant in face of a hostile world. By that suffering he saved truth for his people and his people for the truth. By his stripes they were healed.

Jesus, we believe, took that precedent as his own clue to Messianic action. Messianic action was for him an obedience to the divine mind and became for those who loved him the key to the divine nature. So there is pathos in the very nature of God, a divine *kenosis* happening in Christ. What Jesus does is expressive of who God is and a Cross is the focal point of the revelation.

In their different ways, Peter and Paul had vividly known the remaking power of this faith – Peter after shattering betrayal and Saul after bitter antagonism. They talked, within the mother city of a Church steadily making that faith its own, though no Scriptures as yet existed to enshrine it. They were yet to come, born out of the community of this apostolic memory and mind. Here, to be documented in the fruits of retrospect and in present, pastoral tasks, in Gospels and Epistles, was the truth that made the Church.

Whatever they said to each other about their personal experience of despair and crisis, the end of their conversation must surely have been the call of the future. The God whom they confessed through Jesus was 'the God of hope, of patience and of peace'. 'The love of Christ's appearing' was strong upon them – the expectation of *parousia* which neither was to see as a specific event. We cannot require of them perspectives beyond their generation. That the future lay with Christ they had no doubt.

Meanwhile there was the daily present. The grace they had learned in Christ they knew to be uncompulsive. The world, truly, had been redeemed 'by his Cross and precious blood'. But to acknowledge that redemption still required the free surrender of penitence and faith. Paul, in particular, was to wrestle long with the mystery of belief and unbelief. Whence came the hardness and why the openness of hearts? Was there some arbitrary or inscrutable determining of this alternative? Was faith like the old election by which old Israel had understood its relationship with God, only that the will to faith was, now, what the chance of birth had earlier been? Hardly. For this would be to deny the universal range of grace. One would have to say that the personal experience of grace would seem from within like an overwhelming gift which one could only thankfully take, without thereby concluding from outside that it was withheld from any seeker. What was indisputably 'the gift of God', 'not of ourselves', was nevertheless our free and active receiving.

Saul had a sharp experience of the will to self-righteousness, the trap of the cult of merit, and the pride of law-abiding in censure of the law-breakers. This made him acutely aware of the wonder of unmerited grace and jealous for the liberty in Christ. Peter, never having sat at the feet of Gamaliel, had, we may assume, a gentler approach to these psychic tangles of the law. Having sat at the feet of Jesus, Peter was more liable to see the pathos of the prodigal than the paradox of the scribe. Temperamental differences no doubt compounded these characteristics of biography included, as they were, in 'the manifold grace of God' (1 Peter 4:10).

Meanwhile, the sacred stewardship lay upon each as upon all. In that stewardship the promise of the Holy Spirit was theirs. The work of the Spirit, as they knew with Pentecost so recent, must mean the same loving *kenosis* which they had come to understand about all the ways of God. Here, too, the divine would be conditioned by the human. The heavenly ends would recruit the earthly means. Christ in them, not otherwise, would be 'the hope of glory'.

Was it not this conviction which both heartened and hallowed their leave-taking? We can imagine Paul asking and receiving Peter's blessing: 'The God of all grace, who has called you into his eternal glory by Christ Jesus, after that you have suffered a while, make you perfect, stablish, strengthen, settle you. To him be glory and dominion for ever and ever. Amen'. So the arch-disciple to the once arch-enemy.

Paul, lingering in silence, was moved to lengthen his Amen into an answering benediction which the revolving conversation had been slowly forming in his mind. 'The grace of the Lord Jesus Christ, and the love of God, and the fellowship of the Holy Spirit, be with you.'

For who was host and who was guest, important to them when they met, no longer mattered when they parted.

Study Points and Questions

(1) Looking back over 'the fifteen days' have we, in your view, rightly judged their topics? Have we made any serious omissions? How would you have reconstructed the conversation?

(2) 'The place where the Lord thy God shall choose . . . to put his Name there' (Deut. 12:5). '. . . a place and a name . . .' (Isaiah 56:5). Explain how this biblical conviction of God 'encountered' in event passes into the Christian faith as to the Christ event. We learn to 'place' our theology, so to speak, where Jesus was the Christ because 'there' we have learned to say: 'This is the Lord . . . we will be glad and rejoice in his salvation' (Isaiah 25:9).

(3) 'The love of Christ makes up our mind', is a fair way of getting at Paul's meaning in 2 Corinthians 5:14. How does it 'decide' us about God? And about ourselves?

(4) The three Semitic theisms, Judaism, Christianity and Islam, have great doctrines broadly in common – faith as to creation, revelation, law and prophethood. What is the distinctively Christian faith as to God, that is, 'God in Christ', to which these other truths point forward?

(5) How would you understand and explain Paul's meaning in the phrase: 'He emptied himself . . .' (Phil. 2:7)?

(6) What is meant by 'negative theology'? What considerations prompt it? Is it Christian to believe that we can 'be sure' of God? If so, why?

(7) How, for Paul, were 'law' and 'grace' related?

(8) What do you think Peter intended by the phrase 'a faithful Creator' (1 Peter 4:19) and Paul by the phrase 'the God of patience' (Romans 15:5)?

(9) What do you think most people mean when they use the words: 'Almighty God'? What should they mean? Can you have *both* omnipotence and love?